CAMBRIDGE
UNIVERSITY PRESS

ICT Starters

Initial Steps

Victoria Ellis, Sarah Lawrey and Doug Dickinson

CAMBRIDGE
UNIVERSITY PRESS

University Printing House, Cambridge CB2 8BS, United Kingdom

One Liberty Plaza, 20th Floor, New York, NY 10006, USA

477 Williamstown Road, Port Melbourne, VIC 3207, Australia

314–321, 3rd Floor, Plot 3, Splendor Forum, Jasola District Centre, New Delhi – 110025, India

79 Anson Road, #06–04/06, Singapore 079906

Cambridge University Press is part of the University of Cambridge.

It furthers the University's mission by disseminating knowledge in the pursuit of education, learning and research at the highest international levels of excellence.

www.cambridge.org
Information on this title: www.cambridge.org/9781108463515

First published 2003
Second edition 2005
Third edition 2013
Fourth edition 2019

ISBN 978-1-108-46351-5

20 19 18 17 16 15 14 13 12 11 10 9 8 7 6 5 4 3 2 1

Printed in the United Kingdom by Latimer Trend

A catalogue record for this publication is available from the British Library

ISBN 978-1-108-46351-5 Paperback

Additional resources for this publication at www.cambridge.org/9781108463515

Introduction

Cambridge ICT Starters: Initial Steps has been written to support you in your work for the Cambridge International Diploma ICT Starters syllabus (Initial Steps) from 2019. This book provides full coverage of all of the modules so that you will have a good range of skills and information to support you in the next stages of your ICT development. The modules can be studied in any order.

The book supports your work on the key skills needed at this level to become knowledgeable in emailing, handling data, basic spreadsheet management, creating and editing written work and handling images.

The book provides you and your helpers with:

- examples of activities to do
- exercises to practise the skills before you put them into practice
- final projects to show just how much you have learnt
- optional scenario and challenge activities for those who want to challenge themselves further.

It is designed for use in the classroom with help and support from trained teachers. The tasks, skills and activities have been set in real situations where computer access will be essential. At the start of each module there is a section called 'Before you start …' which explains what you need to know before you begin. The activities are designed to lead you towards a final project where you will have the opportunity to display your knowledge and understanding of each of the skills.

Some exercises require you to open prepared files for editing. These files are available to be downloaded by your teachers from www.cambridge.org/ 9781108463515. You will find that the website provides the files to get you started. These files are included to help you start the activities in this book.

The modules in this book use Microsoft Office 2016, Microsoft Paint, Scratch, Gmail and a variety of web browsers and search engines. Using these will develop your digital skills and will mean that the notes and activities in the book will be easy for you to follow. However, your teacher may decide to use different applications to help you to meet the module objectives.

We hope that you will enjoy working on this stage and will take pleasure in your learning.

Good luck!

Contents

Initial Steps

Introduction

How to use this book

In every module, look out for these features:

Module objectives: this table shows you the key things that you will learn in this module.

	In this module you will learn how to:	Pass/Merit	Done?
1	Plan a short sequence of instructions (an algorithm)	P	
2	Create a program as a sequence of instructions.	P	

Key words: these boxes provide you with definitions of words that may be important or useful.

> **Key word**
>
> **Order:** the way items are arranged.

Did you know?: these boxes provide interesting information and opportunities for further research.

> **Did you know?**
>
> Angles are important and you will learn about these in mathematics, too.

Tip: these boxes give you handy hints as you work.

> **Tip**
>
> There are lots of different answers that are all correct.

Stay safe!: these boxes contain important e-safety advice.

> **Stay safe!**
>
> The world wide web can be fun and is full of lots of interesting and entertaining webpages. However, you may also come across some dangers.

Challenge: These activities are more difficult and extend beyond the syllabus.

> **Challenge**

Scenario: These are activities that help you practise everything you have learnt in the module in a "real-life" situation.

> **Scenario**
>
> ## Escape from the castle

Pass/Merit: this shows you the level of all of the activities in the book.

> **Skill 6** **P/M** **M** **P**

Skill box: these boxes contain activities for you to test what you have learnt.

> **Skill 1**

Watch out!: These boxes help you to avoid making mistakes in your work.

> **WATCH OUT!**
>
> Be careful what you choose as your email address. You don't want to tell people private information about you.

	In this module, you will learn how to:	Pass/Merit	Done?
1	Enter simple words, using a keyboard or other device	P	
2	Select and edit text	P	
3	Select basic icons (e.g. print, save or spell check) using the mouse or other pointing device	P	
4	Name, save and retrieve documents	M	
5	Use appropriate methods to check text is error free.	M	

Did you know?

Before computers were invented, people used typewriters to create documents that they did not want to write by hand.

A typewriter let them press a key, like we do on a keyboard. The key would then strike an ink ribbon to make a letter appear on the page.

In this module you are going to develop typing skills to help you work towards your final project. This project will be about writing an article for your school magazine. You will learn:

- the basic skills of word processing
- to type text into a document to create words and sentences
- how to use the buttons on a mouse to select and change text in a document
- how to use some of the many buttons that you can see in Microsoft Word
- how to save your document with a suitable filename
- how to check your text for errors, including using a spellchecker and proofreading.

You will also learn:

- how to stay safe when using a computer
- how to rename a document that you have saved.

Before you start

You should:

- be able to write simple sentences using spaces, full stops and capital letters
- understand what a mouse is
- understand that when you move a mouse it will move a pointer on the computer screen.

Introduction

Word processing is when you create or change electronic documents by typing **text** or changing text in the document. Word processing is a very valuable skill to master.

You will use it many times and for many reasons, from creating school work, to applying for your dream job.

Word-processing skills are used to create electronic documents that you can share with people using email or other electronic methods of communication. Having these skills also means you can save a copy of the document so that you can change it whenever you want.

The word-processing **software** you will use in this module is Microsoft Word. There is other word-processing software available, so you may be using a different one. You will probably find, however, that they all have very similar buttons and **icons** on the buttons.

WATCH OUT!

You need to make sure that you stay safe when using a computer. You should not have any food and drink near you when using one. You could easily spill your drink onto the computer and this could cause an electric shock.

You could also drop food into your keyboard and this may clog the **keys** and stop them working.

You should never touch the wires that plug into your computer. If you have any problems with your computer, you should always tell your teacher.

Skill 1

Using a mouse

You need to use a **mouse** to choose where you want to start typing text and to **select** the text that you want to edit.

When you move your mouse, you will see a **pointer** move on the **screen**.

Key words

Word processing: this is the skill of typing and editing text.

Text: these are the letters and words that appear on screen when you type using the keys on the keyboard.

Software: this is a program that you use on the computer to do different things, such as word processing.

Icon: this is an image, a word, or an image and word together on a button that you can click.

Keys: these are all the things on a keyboard that you can press.

Key word

Mouse: this is part of a computer that you use to move the pointer on the screen.

Select: this is when you highlight some text because you want to edit it.

Pointer: this is the marker that appears on screen to show you where the mouse is.

Screen: this is the part of the computer that lets you see all the text that you have typed.

Cursor: this is a marker on the screen that lets you know where the text will be when you start typing.

A mouse normally has two buttons: a left button and a right button. You will use the left one most of the time. This is the button that you will click to select different things.

You might need to do a single-click to select, or a double-click. A single-click means that you click the mouse button once. A double-click means that you click the mouse button twice. Make sure that you click it twice very quickly.

Activity 1.1

Open a new document by double-clicking on the Microsoft Word icon on your computer's desktop. You should see a blank page on the screen. Find the mouse pointer on the screen.

Move the pointer to the left side of the screen, then across to the right side of the screen. What do you notice about the pointer when it is on the page and off the page?

Move the pointer to the top of the screen, then all the way down to the bottom of the screen.

Activity 1.2

Look for the flashing line at the top left of the document. This flashing line shows where you will start typing text into the document; this is called the **cursor**.

Move the mouse pointer to the middle of the page and double-click the left mouse button. You should see that the cursor has moved from the top of the page to the middle of the page.

Skill 2

Using a keyboard

You can use a keyboard to type text into an electronic document. You need to press the keys on the keyboard so that the text appears on the screen. You will need to learn how to type using lots of different keys.

Typing a word

To type a word, find the letters that are needed for the word on the keyboard and press each letter. You will see each letter appear on the screen to make the word. Letters can also be called **characters**.

When you type a word at the beginning of a sentence or or its own, you might see the first letter of the word change to a **capital letter**. This is because Microsoft Word is often set to change the first letter of every sentence to a capital letter.

Typing capital letters

To make a letter a capital letter, press and hold down the **Shift** key then press the letter you want to type as a capital letter. When you have typed the letter, you can stop pressing the shift key.

You can use the **Caps Lock** key to type more than one letter in capitals. If you press this key, every letter that you press after that will be typed as a capital letter until you press the caps lock key again.

Typing spaces between words and sentences

To create a space between each word, finish typing the word then press the **Space bar** key. The space bar key is normally the big, long key that is at the bottom of your keyboard in the middle.

To create a space between sections of text (for example, to make a new paragraph), finish typing the sentence and press the **Enter** key. This will move the cursor down to the next line of your document so you can write your next paragraph.

Typing punctuation

When you begin typing sentences into your document, you will need to use **punctuation**. The two most common pieces of punctuation that you will need to use are the comma and the full stop.

Enter: this is a key on the keyboard that you can use to move the cursor to the next line.

Punctuation: these are characters such as a comma, a full stop and a question mark.

To type a comma, you need to press the comma key.

To type a full stop, you need to press the full stop key.

On your keyboard, you may see that some keys have a character at the bottom and a character at the top. When you press the key, it is the character at the bottom that will be typed.

If you want to type the character at the top, you need to press and hold the shift key, then press the character key, and the character at the top will be typed.

Activity 2.1

Type the following sentence into your document:

> **I love ICT! It's really good fun and I learn lots of useful skills.**

Make sure you use the correct punctuation.

Activity 2.2

Look back at the 'Typing spaces between words and sentences' section above. Create a new paragraph and type another sentence about your favourite part of ICT.

Make sure that you have a space between your last sentence and your new sentence to show that you have created a new paragraph.

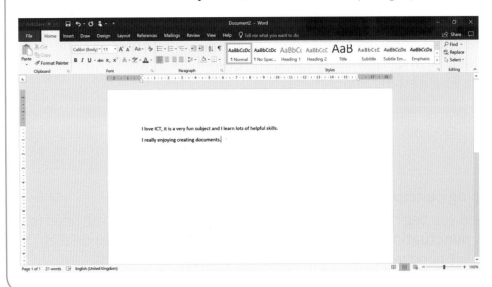

Skill 3

Selecting and editing text

Sometimes when you are typing text you might make a mistake. Sometimes you might decide that you don't like some text that you have typed and want to change it. When you change text, this is called **editing** it.

Deleting text

To edit the text, you might need to **delete** text first. You can delete text one letter at a time, or you can delete a whole word or sentence at once.

To delete text one letter at a time, move the cursor to the right side of the letter that you want to delete and click the left mouse button once. You should see that the cursor is now next to the letter.

Now press the backspace key and you will see that the letter has been deleted. If you keep pressing the backspace key, more letters will be deleted, one by one.

To delete text one word or sentence at a time, select the word or text first. To select text, move the mouse pointer to the right side of the word or sentence that you want to select.

Click and hold down the left mouse button. Move the mouse cursor to the left, to the beginning of the word or sentence that you want to select. Stop clicking the left mouse button now and you should see that the word is **highlighted**. You will be able to tell that it is highlighted as it will have a different colour background.

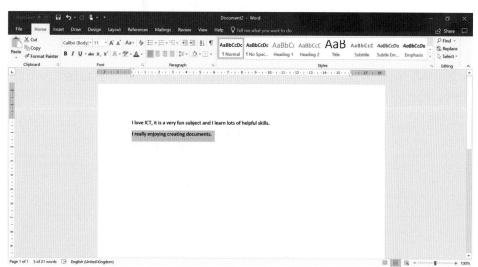

Can you tell which text is selected here?

Key words

Edit: this is when you make changes to text.

Delete: this is when you remove text.

Tip

You can also select a full word by moving the mouse pointer over the word and double-clicking the left mouse button. This will select the full word all at once.

Key word

Highlight: this is when the background colour behind the text changes because you have selected the text.

Menu: this is a box that opens on the screen that gives you a list of options to choose.

Cut: this is when you store the text that you have selected to the clipboard. The text is also removed from the page you do this on.

Clipboard: this is a special storage area on the computer where any text that you cut or copy is put until you need to paste it.

Paste: this is when you put the text that you copied onto the clipboard back onto the page.

You can now press the backspace key to delete the selected text.

You can also select a whole word by putting the mouse pointer anywhere in the word and double-clicking the left mouse button.

Moving text

Sometimes you might have typed some text into your document, but then you decide that it is in the wrong place. You can move text easily if you do this.

To move text, you need to select the text first. When you have selected the text, click the right mouse button. This will open a **menu**. Click on the option '**cut**' in the menu using the left mouse button. This will then remove the text from where it was.

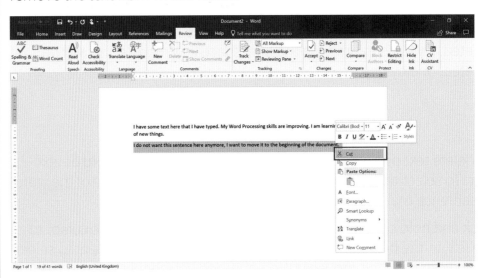

The text has been stored in the computer's **clipboard**. You can now put this text in its new place.

To do this, move the cursor to the place that you want to put the text and click the right mouse button. This will open the menu again.

Click the left mouse button and the first option under the '**Paste**' Options. You will now see the text appear in the new place.

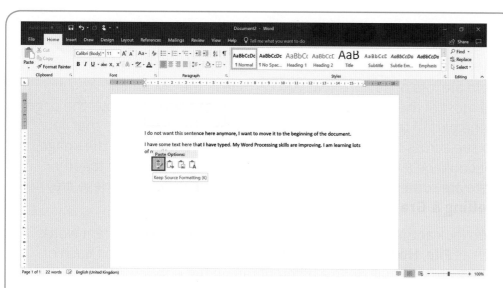

If you have the same text that you want in two different places, then you can use similar instructions to the cut and paste options, but instead of choosing the option 'cut', you choose the '**copy**' option from the menu. This will not remove the text like the cut option, but it will copy the text onto the clipboard.

You can then paste the text in the different place that you wanted it.

Activity 3.1

Delete the word 'fun' letter by letter from your document and type the word 'exciting' in its place.

Activity 3.2

Delete the word 'helpful' as a whole word from your document and type the word 'useful' in its place.

Activity 3.3

Type the following sentence into the end of your document:

'I will move this sentence to show my new word-processing skills.'

Move the sentence that you have just typed to the beginning of the document.

Activity 3.4

Type the following sentence into the end of your document:

'I want to copy this sentence to the beginning of my document.'

Copy the sentence that you have just typed to the beginning of the document.

Key words

Ribbon: this is the area at the top of the page where you can find all the buttons that you can use.

Print: this is what you do to make a paper copy of the document.

Skill 4

Selecting basic buttons

There are lots of buttons that you can see in the document. You will find most of the buttons across the top of the window, above the page, on the part of the screen called the **ribbon**. This is the strip that you can see across the top of the screen. A button could be a little image, or it could be a word. It could also be a word and an image together. There are some buttons that you need to be able to use. These are **Spelling & Grammar**, **Print** and **Save**.

If you look at the top of the ribbon, you may see lots of different words such as **File**, **Home**, **Insert**, **Draw** and **Design**. If you click on each of these words you will open a different tab on the ribbon.

The ribbon has different tabs as it would be extremely difficult to fit all the buttons into one area. Each tab has different buttons to make it easier for you to see them.

Spell check button

When you have typed out text into a document, you should spell check it to see if any words have an incorrect spelling. You can use the **Spelling & Grammar** button to check the spelling of the text you have typed.

You can find the spell check button on the **Review** tab.

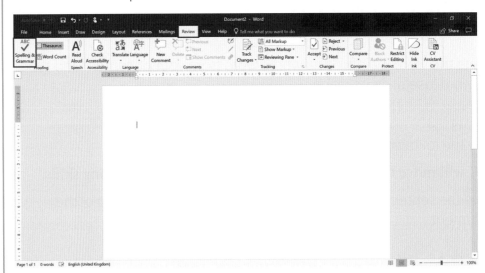

To start a spell check on your document, make sure the cursor is at the start of the document, then click the **Spelling & Grammar** button.

If there are no spelling errors in your document, the spellchecker will tell you that it has checked everything and that no errors were found.

If the spellchecker finds a spelling error in your document, it will open an editor **window** at the right side of the screen. In the window you will be able to choose the correct spelling for the word that you wanted to type.

To choose the correct word, just click on it with the left mouse button. The spellchecker will then move on through the document to the next spelling error, if there are any more.

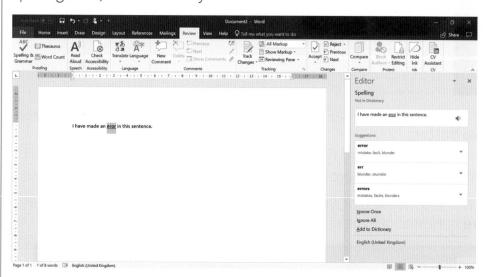

The spellchecker will also check your grammar. So, you may find that it will sometimes give you corrections for this as well.

If you want to close the window when you have finished, click on the cross in the top right corner of the window. Don't click on the cross in the top right corner of the screen as this will close your document completely!

Print button

When you have finished typing your document, you might want to print it out. This could be to store it away for another day, or to give a copy to someone, like your teacher.

To print the document, you will use the **Print** button. You can find the **Print** button on the **File** tab.

Click on the **File** tab, then click on the 'Print' option. This will open a print window that will show you the document that you want to print.

When you are ready to print the document, click on the **Print** button near the top left corner of the screen.

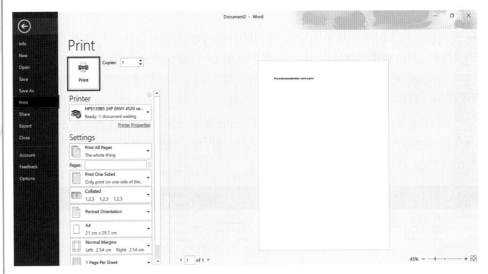

Save button

When you have finished typing your document, you will want to save all your hard work so that you can use it again in the future.

To save your document, you will use the **Save** button. You can find the **Save** button above the ribbon in the top left corner of the screen.

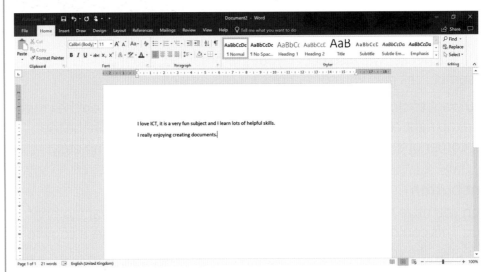

Click on the **Save** button and this will save your document. If it is the first time that you are saving the document, the screen will change to a different window called the 'Save As' window.

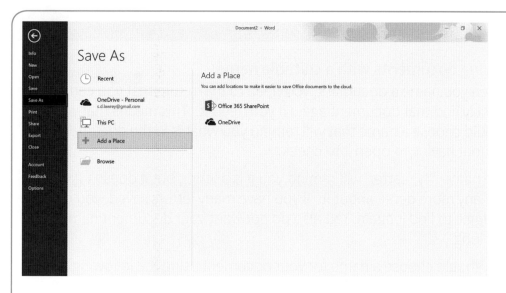

Choose the place where you want to save the file, then type a suitable filename in the box that says 'Enter filename here'. You will learn how to choose a suitable filename in the next skill section. When you have typed a filename, click 'Save'. You may find that Microsoft Word automatically puts the first line of text in your document as a filename. You will need to delete this and type in the suitable filename that you want to use.

Once you have saved the file for the first time, you can click on the **Save** button at any time and save it again. You won't need to type a filename each time, it will save using the first one that you typed.

Activity 4.1
Open the file 'Letter.doc' that your teacher will give you. Spell check the letter to see if there are any errors.

Activity 4.2
Explain to a friend or your teacher how you would print the letter.

Activity 4.3
Save the file using the **Save** button.

Saving documents with a suitable name

When you name a document, you need to make sure that you can quickly find that document again if you need it. This means that you should choose a name that will remind you what is in the document, without having to open it to check.

The name 'My_Letter' will remind you it is a letter, but it doesn't give you any more detail about it. If you have many letters saved, you may struggle to find it again. You also do not want your document name to be too long.

You should choose a name for your document using the following guidelines:

Make sure that it:

- is not too long
- is detailed enough to tell you what is in the document
- does not contain any spaces.

Spaces in a filename make it difficult for some software to read the filename, so this is why you shouldn't use them. Instead of a space, you could use an underscore. This is a small line that can be typed between each word, for example My_Letter. See if you can find the underscore character on your keyboard.

Activity 5.1

You are saving a document that is a letter you have written to your friend. The letter tells your friend about your new word-processing skills. You thought about saving the letter as 'My_Letter' but realise this is not a good filename.

Which of the following filenames would be an improvement? Why would it be an improvement?

MyLetterToMyFriendAboutWordProcessing

Letter_About_WP

LetterToFriend

Why would it be an improvement? Write down your reason.

_____

_____

_____

Why are the other filenames not as good? Write down your reason.

_____

_____

_____

Skill 6

Proofreading text

You have already spell checked your letter, but you can also **proofread** your document to make sure that it has no errors in it.

When you are proofreading you need to think about the following:

- Are all the words correct? Sometimes you may not have misspelt a word, but it might be an incorrect word. For example, you might have wanted to write 'it was a beautiful scene' but instead you typed 'it was a beautiful seen'. The word 'seen' is spelt correctly, but it is not the word that you intended to type.

- Is all the punctuation correct? For example, do all the sentences have a full stop at the end or other appropriate punctuation?

- Are capital letters used correctly? For example, do all sentences and proper nouns (such as a person's name) start with a capital letter?

You can proofread a document on screen, or you can print it out and proofread it.

Activity 6.1

Open the file 'Proofread_Me.doc' that your teacher will give you. Proofread the file, using the guidelines, to see if you can spot any errors. Correct any errors that you find.

Key word

Proofreading: this is when you read through all the text in a document to see if you can find any mistakes.

Bee survival

You have been asked to check a document that your friend has written for a project that you are doing together. The project is about the survival of bees. Your friend has left you with some instructions, including some text that needs editing.

Activity 1

Open the file 'Bees.doc' that your teacher will give you.

Add the following text to the end the file:

> 'This is our project about bees. It shows the information that we have learnt about bees and the importance that they have.'

When you have typed the text, move it to the beginning of the document and make it a new paragraph.

Activity 2

Change the lowercase letter at the beginning of the name 'deeraj' to a capital D.

Activity 3

Spell check the document.

Activity 4

Save the document with a more suitable filename than 'Bees'.

Activity 5

Proofread the document to see if it has any more errors in it.

Challenge

You might find that you want to change the name of a file that you have saved to something more suitable.

To change the name of a file, you need to find the file in your documents.

Activity 1

When you have found the file, click on the file once with the left mouse button. This will select the file.

When you have selected the file, click once with the right mouse button and this will open a menu.

Select the option 'Rename' from the menu. You will see a black box appear around the filename, and the text will be highlighted.

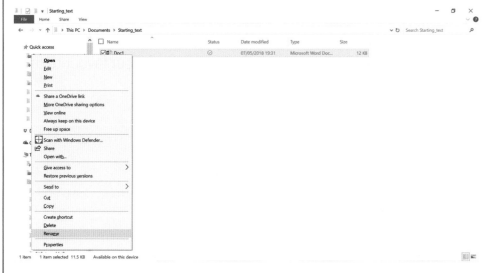

You can now delete the filename and type a new one.

Final project – Your favourite day!

You have been asked by the team working on your school magazine to write an article about your favourite day. You need to use your word-processing skills to type your article to send to the editor.

Activity 1

Open a new Microsoft Word document and write about your favourite day. Think about the following questions:

- Where did you go?
- What did you do?
- Who was with you?
- What made it your favourite day?

Activity 2

Spell check your document when you have finished.

Activity 3

Save your document with a suitable title.

Activity 4

Proofread your document.

Reflection

1 Describe three ways that you will use your new word-processing skills.

_____

_____

_____

_____

2 Describe two ways that you will keep yourself safe when using your word-processing skills.

_____

_____

_____

_____

3 What is good about typing text into a document rather than handwriting it on paper? Write down two benefits.

_____

_____

_____

_____

	In this module, you will learn how to:	Pass/Merit	Done?
1	Use simple shapes and lines to create pictures or patterns	P	
2	Edit pictures, using visual effects	P	
3	Add details to an existing picture, using straight lines or geometric shapes	P	
4	Copy or delete a character or object	**M**	
5	Use 'Save as' to store edited pictures.	**M**	

In this module you are going to develop digital drawing skills to help you work towards your final project. You will learn:

- some very useful and fun image creation and editing skills
- how to use line tools and brush tools and how to draw with them
- how to use the pencil tool (a tool that can be used to do lots of freehand drawing)
- how to create shapes and how to fill them with colour
- how to copy or delete images
- how to save pictures you have edited
- how to develop the skills you need to create a movie character of your own.

You will also learn:

- how to create a shape that has one colour as the border outline and a different colour as the fill.

Before you start

You should:

- be able to use a mouse, including moving the pointer around the screen and using the different buttons
- understand how to choose and open software (programs used on a computer).

Introduction

Creating and **editing** images can be fun. It allows you to create an image exactly how you want it, rather than using images that other people have created for you. It can be very rewarding looking at an image you have designed and made using your skills.

Key word

Edit: making changes to an image.

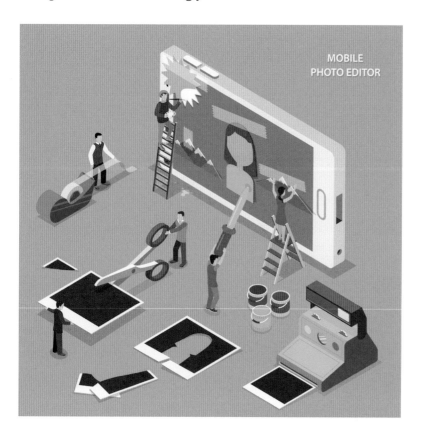

The software that you may use in this module is Microsoft Paint. This is software used for creating and editing **graphics**. It has lots of tools that you will learn to use to help you create images.

There are other image software programs available, so you might be using a different one. You will probably find that they all have very similar buttons and **icons**.

Key words

Graphics: another word for images that are made using computers.

Icon: a small image that you can click.

Key words

Line: this is what you will see when you use a line or brush tool.

Canvas: the white space that you draw on that is like a page.

Skill 1

Using the line tool

The skill of being able to use the **line** tool will mean that you can begin to create lots of different images. This is one of the basic tools of the software.

When you open Microsoft Paint, you will see a big white area. This area is called the **canvas**. It is like the paper that you would draw on if you were creating an image by hand.

This is the canvas.

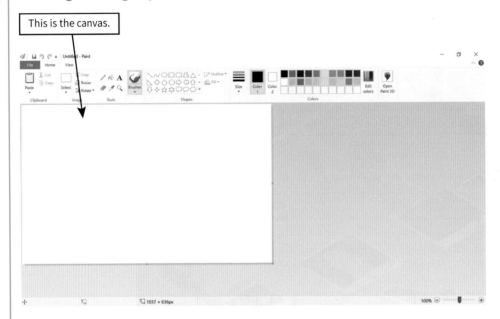

You need to use the straight line tool to draw straight lines. When you can draw straight lines, you can create lots of exciting shapes for your image.

If you don't like the line or shape that you draw, you can remove the last thing that you did using the **undo** tool. If you click on the **Undo** button, it will remove the last line that you drew, or the last thing that you did. If you keep clicking on the **Undo** button, it will keep removing the last things that you did, in the order that you did them.

Key word

Undo: this removes the last thing that you did.

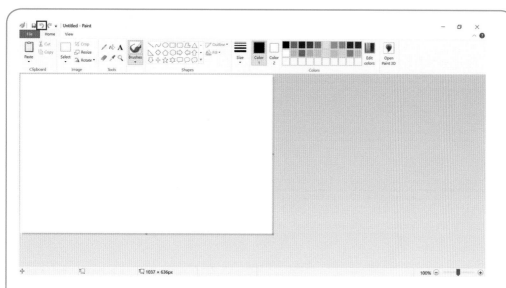

The straight line tool can be found in the shapes section at the top of the page. It is the first tool in the box.

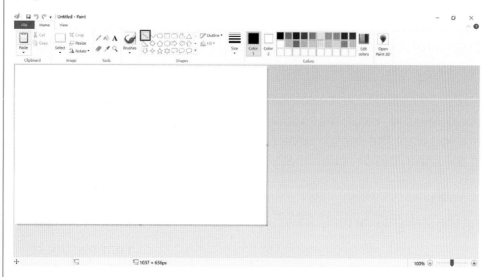

To draw a straight line, click on the **Line tool** button.

Move the mouse pointer to the canvas, to the place where you want the line to start.

Click and hold down the left mouse button to start drawing a line.

Move the mouse across the canvas where you want to draw the line.

Stop clicking on the left mouse button when you get to the point that you want the line to end. You should now see a line drawn on the canvas.

You can create curved lines as well as straight lines. The tool to draw curved lines is next to the line tool in the box.

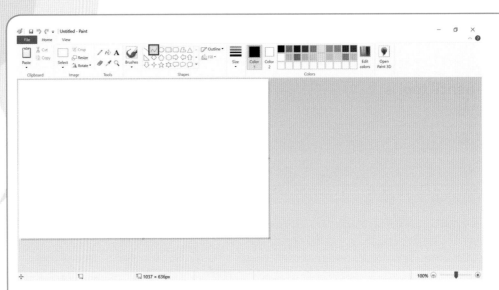

To draw a curved line, click on the curved line tool.

Move the mouse pointer to the canvas, to the place where you want the line to start.

To begin with, draw a line in the same way that you would a straight line. You can then create curves in the line.

Microsoft Paint allows you to create two curves in the line.

To create a curve, move the mouse pointer over the line, to the place where you want the line to curve. Click on the left mouse button and drag the line in the direction that you want to create a curve.

Activity 1.1
Using the straight line tool, draw four straight lines to create a square.

Activity 1.2
Using the curved line tool and the straight line tool, draw a flag like this:

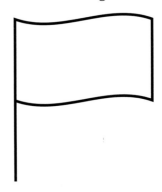

Skill 2

Using the pencil tool

The **pencil tool** is a fun tool to use. It allows you to draw freehand images.

To draw using the pencil tool, click on the **Pencil tool** button.

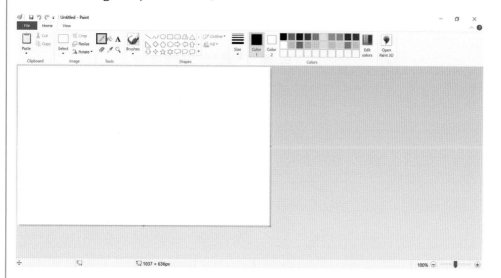

Move the mouse pointer to the canvas, to the place where you want to start drawing.

Click and hold down the left mouse button.

Move the mouse to start drawing with the pencil tool.

You need to move the mouse in the direction that you want to start drawing.

Activity 2.1

Open the file 'Face.png' that your teacher will give you in Microsoft Paint.

Use the pencil tool to make the face into a smiley face.

Activity 2.2

Delete the pencil smile you gave the face and now use the pencil tool to make it into a sad face.

Activity 2.3

Use the pencil tool to draw your favourite flower or an imaginary animal.

Key word

Pencil tool: a tool to draw lines that look like pencil lines.

Tip

It is just like using a pencil on paper: the canvas is like the paper and the mouse acts like a pencil.

Key words

Brush tool: a tool that you can use to draw lines that look like different paint brushes or pens.

Texture: this is the different ways that a line can look from the different brush tools you can use.

Using the brush tool

The **brush tool** is a very creative tool. It allows you to create different **textures** for your drawing. You use it in a similar way to the pencil tool, but you can change the texture to look different from just being a solid line.

To draw using the brush tool, click on the **Brush tool** button.

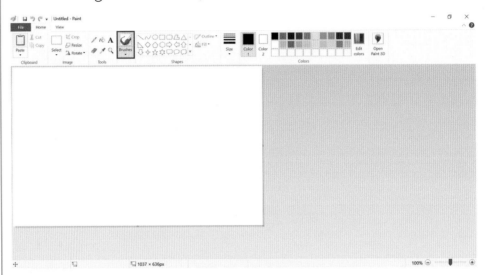

Move the mouse pointer to the canvas, to the place where you want to start drawing.

Click and hold down the left mouse button. Move the mouse to start drawing with the brush tool.

To change the texture of the brush tool, click on the arrow underneath the brush tool and a drop-down **menu** will appear.

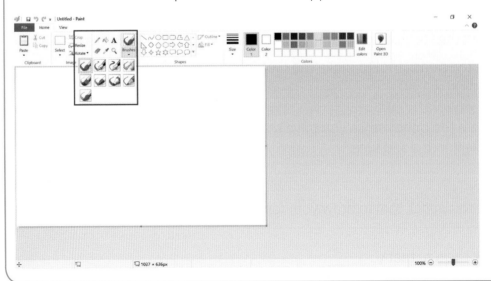

Key word

Menu: a list of options for you to choose.

You can then choose a different texture of brush and draw with it in the same way. Try each one and see what fun textures they create!

Activity 3.1

Open the file 'Shapes.png' that your teacher will give you in Microsoft Paint.

Use the crayon brush tool to colour in the first shape.

Activity 3.2

Use the **airbrush tool** to colour in the second shape.

Activity 3.3

Use the watercolour brush tool to colour in the third shape.

Key word

Airbrush tool: a tool that you can use to draw that looks like spray paint.

Skill 4

Changing the thickness and colour of tools

Changing the thickness of a tool

In your image, you might want some lines to be thick and some lines to be thin.

To do this you need to know how to change the thickness setting of the tool for the lines that you draw.

To change the thickness of the line, click on the **Size** button and a drop-down menu will appear.

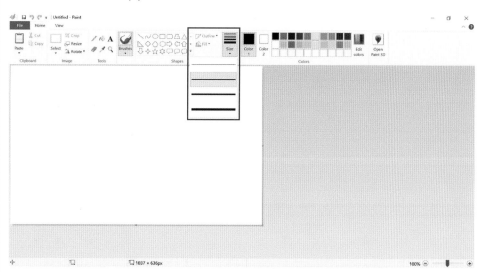

Click the size that you want your line to be, then start drawing your line.

Changing the colour of a tool

You might want to use lots of different colours in your image, so you need to know how to change the colour setting for a tool. You can choose a different colour for your tool from the colours section.

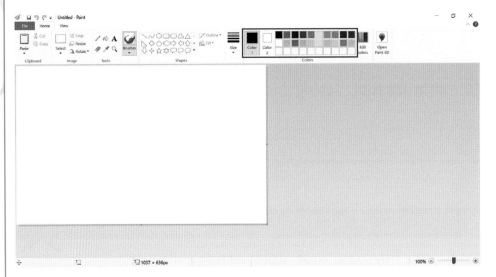

Click the colour that you want to change to and begin drawing your line.

With any of the tools, the colour of the line that you draw will now be the colour you chose.

There are certain colours available to choose in the colour area, but there are more colours than these ones available.

To choose further colours, click the **Edit colours** button.

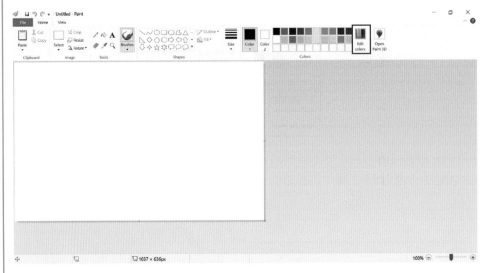

A window will now open with lots more colours that you can choose.

Choose one of the coloured squares on the left, or create a custom colour.

To create a custom colour, click anywhere on the coloured section to the right of the window. This will bring up a line of colour at the right of the window.

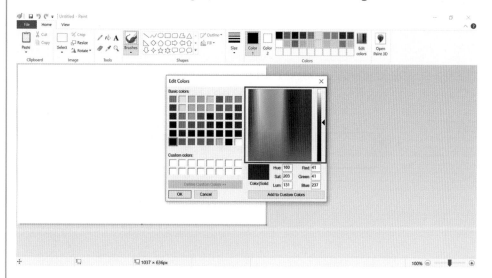

Click at a point on this line for the colour that you want, then click the **Add to Custom Colours** button. The colour will be added to one of the custom colour squares on the bottom left of the window.

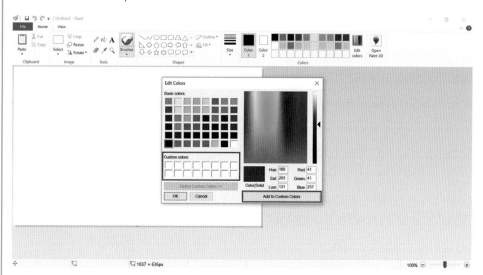

If you now click on the **OK** button, you should see the colour that you chose appear at the bottom of the colours section.

Activity 4.1

Draw four horizontal straight lines, one on top of the other with a small space between each.

Make the first line very thin, then make each line after that thicker.

Activity 4.2

Using either a brush tool or a line tool, draw a rainbow, changing the colour of the tool each time.

Drawing shapes

As well as drawing different kinds of line, you can also draw lots of different kinds of shapes.

To draw a shape, click the shape that you want to draw. You will find all the different shapes that you can use in the shapes area.

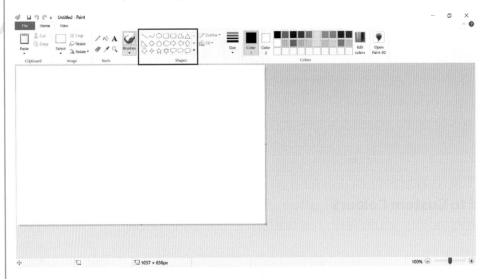

When you have clicked on the shape you want to draw, move the mouse pointer to the canvas.

Click and hold down the left mouse button, then drag the mouse pointer in the direction that you want to draw the shape.

The shape should now appear. Stop clicking the left mouse button when the shape is at the size that you want it.

You can change the colour of a shape using the **fill** tool. This will fill the inside of the shape with the colour that you choose.

Choose the colour you want your shape to be, then click the fill tool.

Key word

Fill: to make the inside of a shape a solid colour.

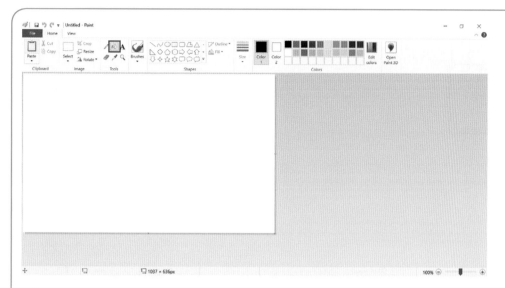

When you move the mouse pointer to the canvas, you should see that it looks like a little paint can. This is how you can tell that you have selected the fill tool.

You can then move the mouse pointer to the middle of the shape that you want to fill and click the left mouse button.

You should now see that the shape is the colour that you chose.

Activity 5.1

Draw three different shapes.

Fill the first shape with red.

Fill the second shape with yellow.

Fill the third shape with green.

Skill 6

Using copy, paste and removing parts of an image

You may want to create a **copy** of a part of your image. You will do this if you want something to appear more than once in your image.

To copy part of your image, you need to select it first. You can do this either by using the rectangular **selection** tool or the free-form selection tool.

Key words

Copy: to save all or part of an image that has been selected into an area called a clipboard, so that it can be pasted when needed.

Select: this is a tool that you can use to draw a box or line around all or part of an image.

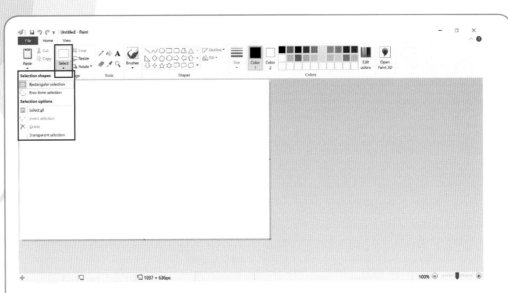

Tip

If the part that you want to copy is a square or a rectangle, the rectangular selection tool will be best.

If the part is any other shape, the free-form tool will be best.

Tip

When using the free-form selection tool, you will need to make sure that the end of the line that you draw touches the beginning of it.

Key word

Paste: to put a copied part of on image back onto the canvas.

Click on the tool that you want to use to select the part of the image that you want to copy.

Move the mouse pointer next to the part of the image that you want to copy.

Click and hold down the left mouse button. If you are using the rectangular selection tool, then move the mouse to place the rectangle around the part you want to copy.

If you are using the free-form selection tool, draw a line around the part of the image that you want to copy.

You should now see a box around the part of the image that you have selected.

You can now click on the **Copy** button to copy the part of the image. It will copy it to the clipboard where it will be stored until you use the **paste** tool.

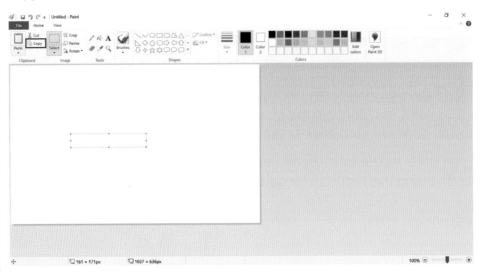

The paste tool allows you to place a copy of what you selected onto a different part of the canvas.

To paste what you selected, move the mouse pointer to where you want to paste, then click on the **Paste** button.

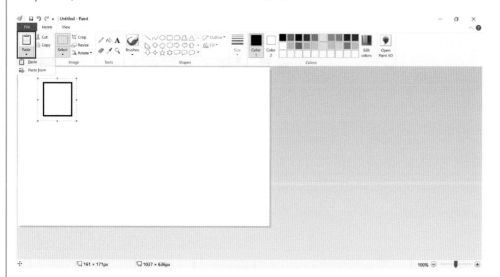

You will now see what you selected pasted onto the canvas.

If you want to delete or move the part of the image that you selected from the canvas, you can do this by using the **cut** tool.

Click on the **Cut** button and it will delete the part of the image that you selected. If you wanted, you could now paste it onto a different place on the canvas.

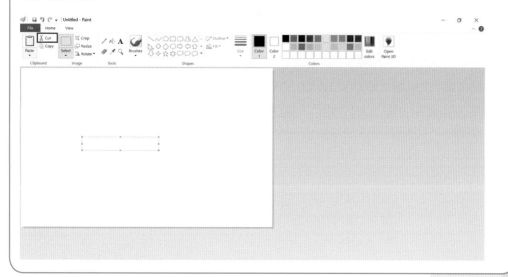

Key word

Cut: to delete all or part of an image that has been selected.

Eraser tool

You can also use the eraser tool to remove parts of your image. The eraser tool is a bit like the eraser that you use to rub out pencil lines when you are drawing on paper.

To use the eraser tool you need to select it first.

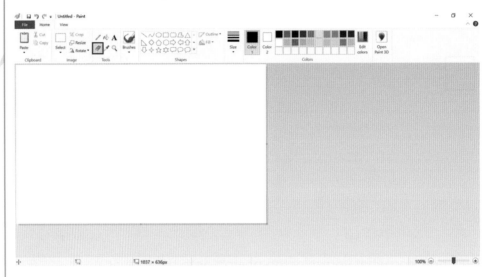

Move your mouse pointer to the part of the image that you want to erase and click and hold the left mouse button.

Move your mouse pointer across the image, just as you would if you wanted to erase something on a piece of paper.

Activity 6.1

Open the file 'Bee.png' that your teacher will give you.

Select the bee and copy it.

Paste the copy of the bee twice to create three bees.

Use a brush tool to add a blue sky behind the bees.

Skill 7

Saving your image

When you create a new image, you need to save it. To save the document, click on the **Save** button. The first time you save a document it will ask you to give it a name.

Click on the **File** button, then click the words '**Save as**'.

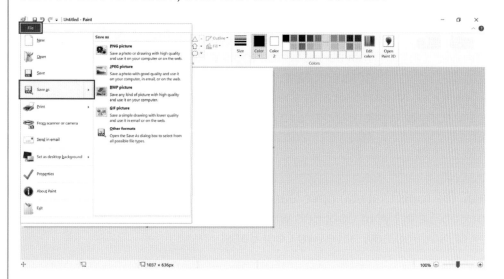

A window will appear and you will need to type a filename for your image. You should choose a filename that will help you easily identify the image if you need it again. When you have typed a filename, click the **Save** button. Your image will now be saved!

Activity 7.1

Open the file 'House.png' that your teacher will give you.

A rectangle has been drawn already in this file.

Add further shapes and lines to the rectangle to make it into a house.

Activity 7.2

Use a brush tool to add the sky and grass to your house image.

Use a shape to add a sun into the sky.

Activity 7.3

Save your house image with a suitable filename.

Key word

Save as: this is what you use to save an image for the first time. It allows you to give the image a name.

Draw Cool Bob

Meet our little character Cool Bob. He is just so funny and silly. You are going to use your excellent image creating skills to draw Cool Bob. He looks like this:

Activity 1

Find a partner and look at the image of Cool Bob. Talk about which tools you could use to draw the different parts of Cool Bob. Remember that you can use line tools, brush tools and shape tools to create him. You can also use the copy and paste tools. See if you can see where you could use them.

Activity 2

Use all the tools that you have learnt about to draw your own version of Cool Bob. Select your Cool Bob when you have drawn him and create a copy of him. You now have two Cool Bobs!

Activity 3

Save your Cool Bob with a suitable filename.

Challenge

It is possible to set one colour as the border outline colour for a shape and a different colour as the fill colour for a shape. You can do this using the Colour 1 and Colour 2 options. Colour 1 is the border outline colour and Colour 2 is the fill colour.

Click the Colour 1 tool and then click the colour that you want for the outline of the shape. Click the Colour 2 tool and then click the colour that you want for the fill of the shape.

You can now draw the shape and it will have the colours that you chose for the outline and the fill.

Activity 1

Draw a square that has a yellow fill and a blue outline.

Draw a circle that has a purple fill and an orange outline.

Tip

The brush will use Color 1 when you click the left mouse button and Color 2 when you click the right mouse button.

Final project – At the movies!

You have been asked by your teacher to create an image of a character from your favourite movie.

You should use the shape, brush and line tools to create the image.

Activity 1

Open a new Microsoft Paint document and use the shape, brush and line tools to draw an image about your favourite movie. Remember that to draw a line or a shape to match one you have already drawn, you can use your copy and paste skills.

Activity 2

Use the fill tool to make your image bright and colourful.

Activity 3

Save your document with a suitable filename.

Reflection

1 How will you use your new skills in image creation? List three examples.

_____

_____

_____

2 Why would you use copy and paste to make a copy of part of your picture, rather than just drawing it again?

_____

_____

3 Look again at the images you have created. What would you do to improve them?

_____

_____

_____

_____

	In this module, you will learn how to:	Pass/Merit	Done?
1	Store information and sort it into groups	P	
2	Show information in charts or graphs	P	
3	Use charts or graphs to answer simple questions	P	
4	Make simple conclusions from charts or graphs.	M	

In this module you are going to develop data handling skills to help you work towards your final project. You will learn how to collect data and make graphs from the data using a program called Microsoft Excel. In the final project you will use your new skills to collect data about your friends' hobbies and create graphs about what they like to do.

You will also learn:

- how to put data into groups (classify it)
- how to create a graph or chart
- how to format a graph or chart
- how to add axis labels to a graph or chart
- how to make conclusions from a chart or graph.

Before you start

You should:

- have used a keyboard to enter data, and used a mouse (or touch screen) to select options
- know that a data table has titles (headings)
- know that the data used in the table is organised under the headings.

Introduction

A **graph** is an image that shows numerical **information** (information about the numbers of things). There are lots of different types of graphs.

In the **bar chart** (at the top of the next page), green is the highest bar, which means it has the greatest number.

In the **pie chart** (beneath the bar chart), green is the largest slice, which means it has the greatest number.

Key words

Graph: a diagram that shows numerical information in a visual way.

Information: a fact about something or someone.

Bar chart/ graph: a graph with vertical bars that shows how many items there are.

Pie chart/ graph: a graph where the whole circle is the grand total, and each slice is a part of the whole.

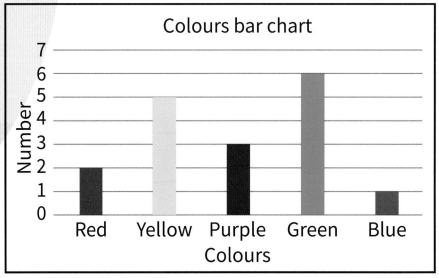

Colours bar chart

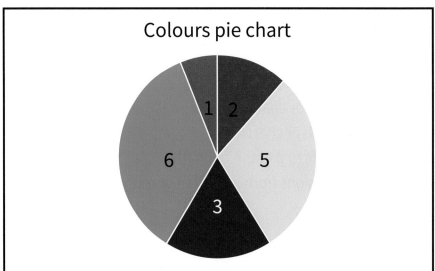

Colours pie chart

Skill 1

Classifying information

Classifying data means arranging it into groups.

One hobby that your friend has is reading. Think about how you could **sort** your friend's books.

For example, they could be put into these groups:

- the colour of the front cover
- the name of the author
- the type of book (for example fiction or non-fiction).

Can you think of other ways you could classify (sort) them?

Activity 1.1

Look at the image below.

How could you group the items in this picture?

One way is to sort them by type of animal. In this case, the groups would be: giraffe, lion and penguin.

Tip

There are lots of different answers that are all correct.

Look at the image showing fruit.

The fruit can be grouped in lots of ways.

Two ways are types of fruit, or colour.

1 Write the names of all the different types of fruit in the image.

_____

2 Write the names of all the different colours in the image.

_____

_____

These are both correct ways of classifying the information in the image.

3 Write any other ways of grouping the fruit that you can think of.

_____

_____

Activity 1.3

Draw a set of different mathematical shapes on a piece of paper, cut them out and sort them in two different ways.

Skill 2	

Counting information

When your data is in groups (classified), you can count how many pieces of information are in each group. This is the total number of items for that group.

There are different ways of counting information, such as using a tally or creating a data table.

Activity 2.1

A tally chart helps you keep track when you have a lot of items to count.

When counting items, put a | for each item. When you reach five, put a line through the four lines, like this:

$$\cancel{||||}$$

It is easier to count up in fives than trying to count lots and lots of single lines.

How many does | | | represent? _____

How many does | represent? _____

Activity 2.2

A tally chart shows all the different groups that you are counting. It has space for you to write the tally for the number of images.

The table has the groups for the animals in this picture.

Use a tally to count how many of each animal is in the picture.

Animal	Tally
Giraffe	
Lion	
Penguin	
Tiger	
Elephant	

Activity 2.3

A data table shows how many animals are in each group.

Complete it by adding each tally and writing the number. This gives you the total.

Use your tally from **Activity 2.2** to write the total number of each animal in the table.

Animal	Total
Giraffe	
Lion	
Penguin	
Tiger	
Elephant	

Activity 2.4

Complete the data table for the fruit in the picture.

1 Write the names of all the different colours in column 1.

2 Add the tally for each colour in column 2.

3 Write the total for each colour in column 3.

Colour (1)	Tally (2)	Total (3)

Pictogram: a word or phrase that is shown using pictures instead of words. In a graph pictogram, images are used to represent objects.

Creating a pictogram

A **pictogram** uses pictures to represent (show) data. One picture can be for one or more pieces of data. For example, one picture could mean ten lions. A pictogram has a key to show what each picture represents. For example two lions would be represented by:

Key

 = one lion

You can create a pictogram of the fruit in this picture by:

1 writing down the groups of fruit
2 drawing the same number of images of each fruit as there are in the picture. There are three bananas so you need three pictures of bananas.

Key

One image = one fruit

Activity 3.1

What does the following pictogram represent?

Key

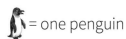= one penguin

Activity 3.2

On a piece of paper, draw a pictogram to represent three apples.
Remember to add a key.

Activity 3.3

On a piece of paper, draw a pictogram to show the number of animals in
this picture.

Tip

Pictograms can
be horizontal
or vertical and
should have
a title.

Tip

Don't worry
about your
drawings. This
isn't an art test!

Microsoft Excel: a piece of software that uses spreadsheets to enter data, perform calculations and create graphs and charts.

Cell: one rectangle in a spreadsheet.

There are lots of different types of spreadsheet software, for example, Numbers in iWorks.

Using Microsoft Excel to create tables

Microsoft Excel is a spreadsheet program.

A spreadsheet program is a special type of software that lets you work with numbers. You can enter data into it.

It can do your maths for you too (if you know the correct commands).

A spreadsheet is made of lots of rectangles called **cells**.

You can write text in a cell by clicking on it and then typing in it.

To write in a different cell, you can click on it and then type in the cell.

This is one cell.

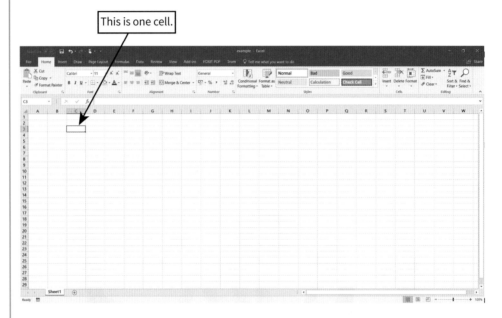

Activity 4.1

Your class is doing a topic on healthy eating and you and your friends have been asked to bring an item of fruit to add to the 'healthy eating' table.

The picture shows the fruit collected by the class.

Your teacher has asked you to represent the fruit in a graph. Your teacher will give you the file 'colours_1.xlsx'.

Open this file.

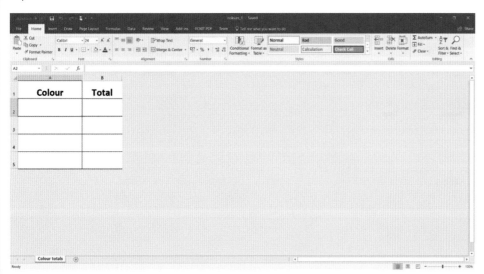

Enter the names of each colour shown in the picture in column A. Each colour should be in a new cell.

Enter the total number of each colour in column B.

Activity 4.2

Your class is going on a visit to the zoo. Your teacher asks all of you to draw the animal that you would most like to see.

The picture below shows the set of animals that was drawn by the class.

Your teacher will give you the file 'zooAnimals.xlsx'.

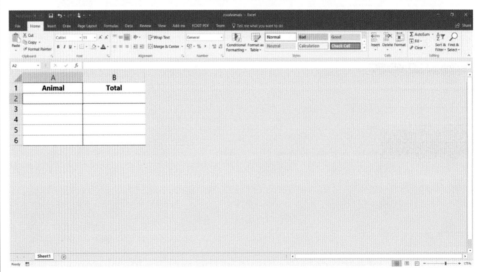

Write the names of the animals in the image in column A.

Write the total number of each animal in the image in column B.

Activity 4.3

You can make pictograms in Microsoft Excel as well.

You are going to make a pictogram for the number of animals in this image.

Your teacher will give you the file 'animals_1.xlsx'.

Open this file.

Drag the pictures of the animals to the boxes to show how many of each animal are in the picture above.

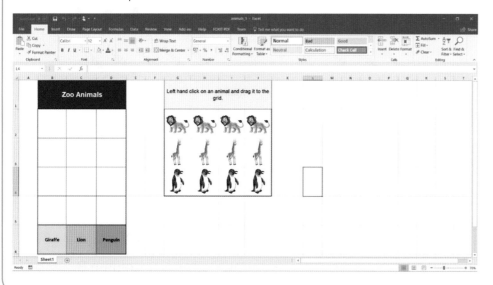

What is a graph?

Graphs are used to make complicated data easier to understand.

This graph below shows how many umbrellas were sold in a shop in India over a year.

The **vertical axis** (the *y*-axis) shows how many were sold.

The **horizontal axis** (the *x*-axis) shows each month.

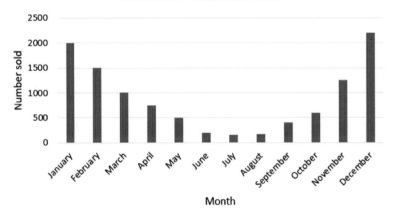

Key words

Vertical axis: this is the axis up the left side of the bar chart (the *y*-axis).

Horizontal axis: this is the axis along the bottom of the bar chart (the *x*-axis).

Tip

It is a good idea to write in full sentences in all of your answers, for example, 'The data shows that…'

Activity 5.1

In which month(s) were the most umbrellas sold?

_____

In which month(s) were the fewest umbrellas sold?

_____

Activity 5.2

What other information can you see from the graph?

Do the bars go up and down in a pattern? Or are they all mixed up?

_____

Activity 5.3

Imagine you own a shop in India. You are thinking about selling umbrellas.

In which months do you need to have the most umbrellas to sell?

_____

Skill 6

Adding data to a graph

You can create a graph from the data in a spreadsheet.

You first need a data table. Here is a spreadsheet:

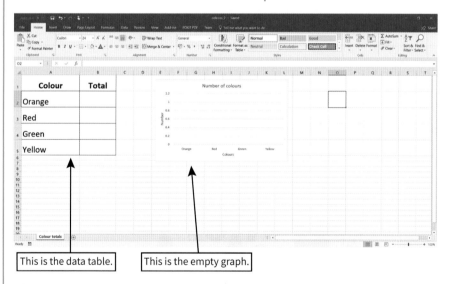

This is the data table.   This is the empty graph.

There is a data table and an empty graph.

The graph is empty because there is no data in the table.

When you enter data into the table, the graph will change.

Activity 6.1

Open the file 'colours_2.xlsx' that your teacher will give you.

Tip
Don't worry about the numbers on the axis, these will change when you enter your totals.

Enter the following numbers into the table:

Orange – 2

Red – 6

Green – 8

Yellow – 1

1 Describe what happened to the graph.

_____

_____

2 Write down the changes that happen to the graph.

_____

_____

Activity 6.2

Change the numbers of the fruit – you can put in any numbers you want.

1 Describe what happened to the graph.

_____

_____

2 Write down the changes that happen to the graph.

_____

_____

Activity 6.3

This picture shows lots of shapes. There are five different types of shapes shown here.

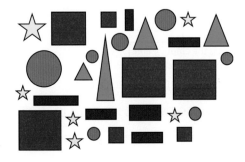

Your teacher will give you the file 'shapes_1.xlsx'.

Open the file.

Complete the data table in the file to create the graph.

Skill 7

Choosing a type of graph

There are different types of graph.

Each graph has its own purpose, for example when it should and shouldn't be used.

For this module you only need to know about two types of graphs: bar graphs and pie charts.

Bar graphs

A bar graph shows how many of something there are.

It has two **axes:**

- *x*-axis (along the bottom of the graph – horizontal)
- *y*-axis (up the side of the graph – vertical).

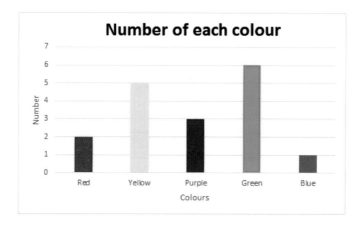

Pie charts

A pie chart shows you what **proportion** of the **grand total** each item is. The whole circle is the total number, then each slice is a proportion of the grand total. The picture below shows a pie chart.

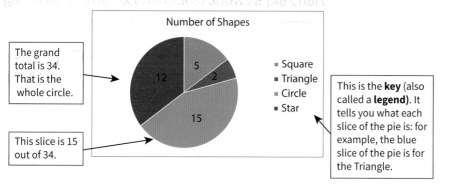

A lot of data can be shown in both bar graphs and pie charts.

Activity 7.1

Find out how many people in your school wear glasses, and how many do not.

1 Would you show this information as a bar graph or a pie chart?

_____

_____

2 Why did you choose this one?

_____

_____

Activity 7.2

Find out how many portions of vegetables each member of your class ate in the last week.

1 Would you show this information as a bar graph or a pie chart?

_____

_____

2 Why did you choose this one?

_____

_____

Skill 8

Creating a graph from a data table

Before you can create a graph, you need to highlight the whole data table, including the titles.

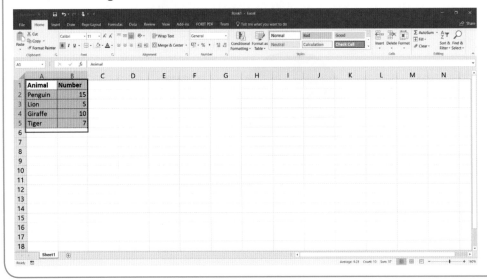

Then click on **Insert** at the top of the screen.

You can click on the **icon** that shows the graph you want. You are going to use the bar graph.

Key word

Icon: a picture on a computer that, when clicked, will perform an action.

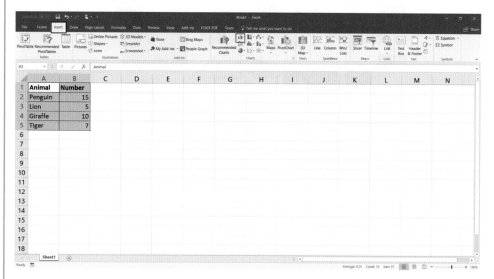

If you click on the bar graph, a menu appears. Choose the first option.

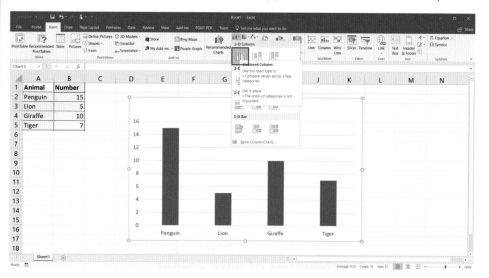

Activity 8.1

Your teacher will give you the file 'shapes_2.xlsx'.

Open the file.

Complete the data table for this picture.

1 Write the names of the shapes in column 1.

2 Write the total number of each shape in column 2.

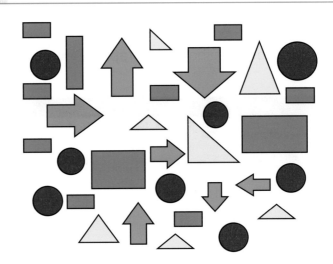

Tip

Remember to highlight the whole table, including the titles.

Activity 8.2

Create a bar graph for the data table you have just completed.

Activity 8.3

Create a pie chart for the same data table you have just completed.

You should now have one bar graph and one pie chart.

Save this file to use later for **Activity 9.4.**

Skill 9

Adding the x-axis, y-axis and titles to a graph

When you have created a graph, you need to make sure it has appropriate titles and labels.

A bar graph needs a title to tell you what the graph is about.

It has two axes. Each axis needs a label.

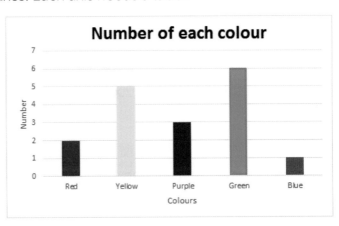

A pie chart has a title. This tells you what the chart is about. A pie chart does not have axes, but should have a key (Microsoft Excel will do this automatically for you).

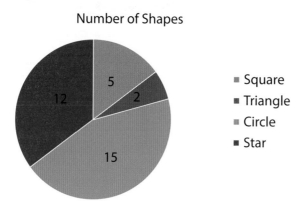

Number of Shapes

To add a new title to a bar graph or a pie chart:

1 Click on the graph.

2 Click, or double-click on the title.

3 Delete the text.

4 Write your new title.

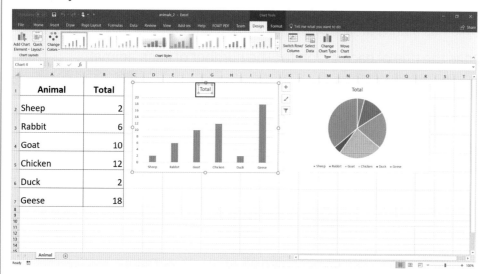

To add axis labels to a bar graph:

1 Click on the **Design** tab.

2 Click on the **Add Chart Element** button.

3 Click on 'Axis Titles'.

4 Choose 'Horizontal' to add an *x*-axis label.

5 Choose 'Vertical' to add a y-axis label.

You can then click on the label, delete the text and add your own.

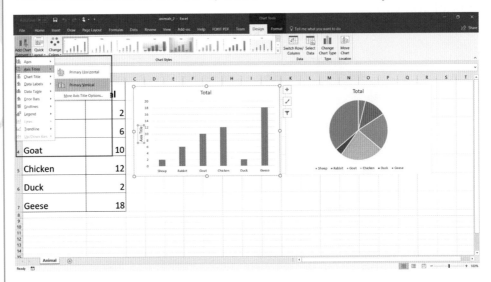

Activity 9.1

Your teacher will give you the file 'animals_2.xlsx'.

Open the file.

The file has a data table and two graphs: a bar graph and a pie chart.

Change the title of each graph to 'The number of each animal'.

Activity 9.2

Add an x-axis label to the bar graph.

Give it the title 'Animals'.

Activity 9.3

Add a y-axis label to the bar graph.

Give it the title 'Number'.

Activity 9.4

Add titles and axes to the graphs you made in **Skill 8**.

Tip

Make sure all the titles describe what the graphs show. Make sure all the axes describe what the data is.

Skill 10

Drawing conclusions from a graph

Graphs let you view data more easily than looking at tables of numbers.

Key word

Conclusion: a decision or statement that is made using information.

Bar graph

- The highest bar is the item that has the largest number.
- The lowest bar is the item that has the smallest number.
- If the bars are very close in height, then there is not much difference between them.
- If the bars change a lot (with some being very high, and others low) then there is more of a difference between them.

Pie chart

- The largest slice is the item that has the largest number, or the largest proportion.
- The smallest slice is the item that has the smallest number, or the smallest proportion.

Activity 10.1

Use the graph to answer the questions.

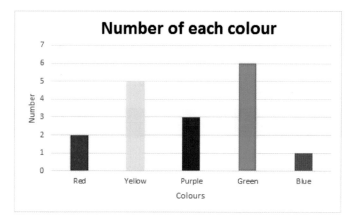

1 Which of these colours has the largest number? _____

2 Which of these colours has the smallest number? _____

3 List the colours from the largest number to the smallest number.

_____

_____

Tip

Which is the highest bar?

Tip

Which is the smallest bar?

Activity 10.2

Use the pie chart to answer the questions.

Number of Shapes

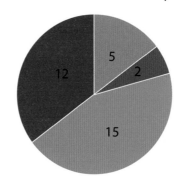

- ■ Square
- ■ Triangle
- ■ Circle
- ■ Star

1 Which shape has the highest number?

_____

2 Which shape has the smallest number?

_____

3 Which shape has the largest proportion of the pie?

_____

4 List the shapes from the smallest number to the highest number.

_____

_____

Tip

Look for the largest slice of the pie, then look at the key.

Tip

It is the same as the highest number.

Scenario

Favourite lessons

Your teacher wants to know what the favourite lesson of the members of your class is.

Activity 1

Create a data table to store these subjects:

  IT, History, Geography, Maths, Other

Add two more subjects of your choice.

Activity 2

Ask the members of your class what their favourite lesson is.

Write the totals in your data table.

Activity 3

Decide if a bar graph or pie chart is most appropriate.

Create a graph or chart to show the favourite lesson of each member of the class.

Activity 4

Add a useful title for your graph.

If you have created a bar graph, add axis labels.

If you have created a pie chart, add a key (unless your version of Microsoft Excel has done this automatically).

Activity 5

Answer the following questions:

1 Which lesson is the most common?

_____

2 Which lesson is the least common?

_____

3 Are there any lessons that are liked by a similar (or the same) number of people?

_____

4 Is there one lesson that more than half the class like the most?

_____

Challenge

Changing the bar colours

Activity 1

You can change the colours of the bars (or pie slices) on a graph.

Change the colour of the bar by clicking on it, twice. (The first click selects the graph, the second click selects the bar.)

It will have a circle in each corner of the bar.

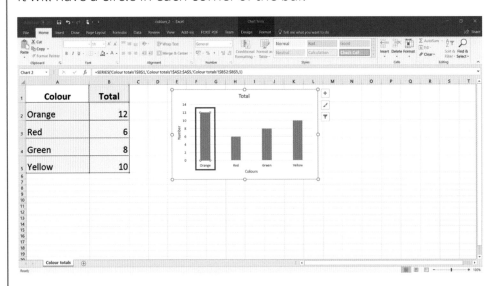

Right-click on the bar. The format menu will appear.

'Fill' lets you change the background colour.

'Outline' lets you change the line around the bar.

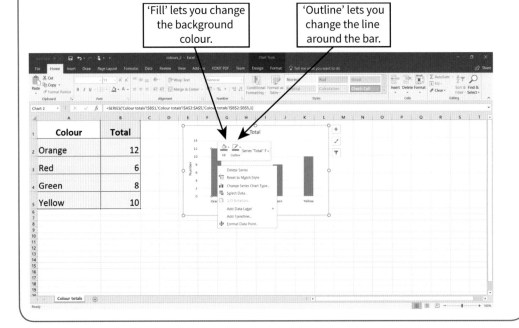

Repeat this with each bar.

This works the same for a pie chart. Click twice on the section of the pie to change its colour.

Changing axes

Activity 2

You might have a graph where the information is squashed together and you can't read the data very well, like this graph.

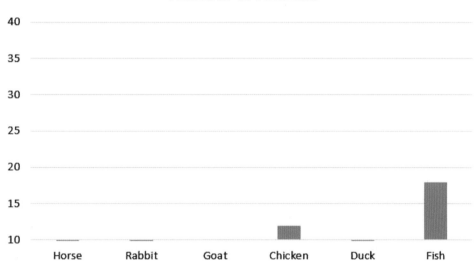

You can change the numbers on the *y*-axis.

Click on the *y*-axis (the vertical numbers up the side of the graph).

Right-click and select 'Format Axis'.

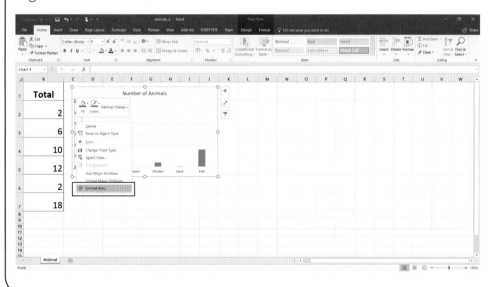

A new window will appear.

Click on the **graph** button.

Change the numbers.

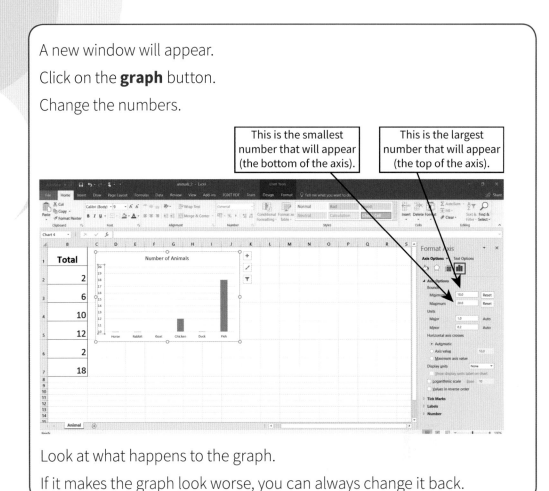

This is the smallest number that will appear (the bottom of the axis).

This is the largest number that will appear (the top of the axis).

Look at what happens to the graph.

If it makes the graph look worse, you can always change it back.

Final project – Creating graphs about your friends' hobbies

Some people have lots of hobbies (things they like doing in their spare time).

For example, some people like to read, some people like to play computer games and some people like cooking.

You will need to find out what the answers to the following questions are:

1 Are there more people who have a favourite hobby of reading than playing computer games?

2 Is the favourite hobby of people in your class playing sport?

3 Do more people have a favourite hobby of reading comics or novels?

4 Do more people have a favourite hobby of watching TV or playing computer games?

Activity 1

Find out what the favourite hobby is of each person in your class (they can only choose one).

Create a data table to show the results you have found.

Create a pie chart to show the favourite hobbies of the people in your class.

Look at your pie chart and answer the four questions above.

Activity 2

Collect data about *all* the different hobbies of each member of your class (they can choose more than one this time).

Create a data table to show the results you have found.

Create a bar chart to show the hobbies that people in your class like.

Make up some questions about your data. Answering these creates information about your data.

Key word
Collect: to gather together.

Tip
Remember to give the chart a useful title.

Reflection

Think about the following:

1 Have you ever made a graph on paper? What did this graph show?

_____

_____

_____

_____

2 What was the difference between making a graph on paper and making a graph on the computer?

_____

_____

_____

_____

_____

3 A school creates a graph of the number of students who are absent each day during a school year.

How could the school use this graph? What information could it tell them?

_____

_____

_____

_____

	In this module, you will learn how to:	Pass/Merit	Done?
1	Plan a short sequence of instructions (an algorithm) to achieve a specific goal	P	
2	Create a program as a sequence of instructions to achieve a particular goal	P	
3	Predict what a Sprite will do when given a sequence of instructions	P	
4	Create a program to: move a Sprite at least 5 times turn a Sprite through angles other than 90 and 180 degrees	M	
5	Correct (debug) a program containing one error.	M	

In this module you are going to develop programming skills to help you work towards your final project. This project will involve using a computer program called Scratch to help Clip Clop the Horse make a journey to visit all the animals in a zoo.

You will also learn:

- what an algorithm is, how to make one and how to correct (debug) one
- how to predict what a Sprite will do when you give it a set of instructions
- how to move a Sprite in Scratch
- how to turn a Sprite in Scratch
- how to make the Sprite say messages in Scratch.

Before you start

You should:

- know that people, and things, can move in lots of different directions – up, down, left and right
- have used angles before:
  - 90 degrees (quarter turn)
  - 180 degrees (half turn)
  - 360 degrees (full turn)

Did you know?

Every time you click a button on a computer or type a letter on the keyboard, instructions stored on the computer tell it what to do. Without these instructions, a computer would just be a box that does nothing.

- know what a sequence is
- have followed sequences to carry out tasks, or solve a problem.

For example, follow this simple sequence:

1 Jump up and down four times.

2 Sit on the floor.

3 Clap your hands three times.

4 Stand up.

5 Turn around.

Introduction

Computers run **programs** called **software**.

The programs are made with lots of **instructions** or **commands** that tell the computer what to do.

The instructions are written in **program code**.

Skill 1

Being a robot

You are going to pretend to be a robot.

You need to:

- stand up
- look around you
- walk to the door.

How would you describe this using a set of clear instructions?

Activity 1.1

Write down the instructions to get to the door.

Your instructions could be:

- turn around to face the front of the room
- walk forward three steps
- turn left
- walk forward one step.

Follow your own instructions: did you make it to the door?

If you didn't get to the door, change your instructions and try again.

Keep on doing this until you can get to the door.

Well done! That's your first sequence of instructions.

Activity 1.2

Following your own instructions can be easy, because you wrote them. This time, swap places with a friend. Give your friend your instructions to use, and you use their instructions. Follow these instructions and see if you can make it to the door. Did your friend make it, too?

WATCH OUT!
Be careful of other people while doing this!

Skill 2

Moving a robot through a maze

Imagine you are a robot following instructions to get through a maze.

Look at this maze.

You need to start in the green box with 'START' written in it.

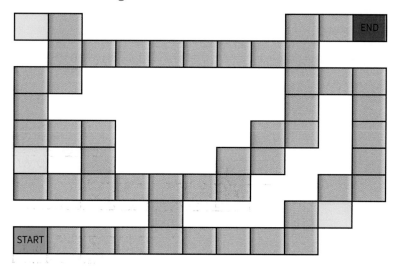

Each coloured box is one space. You can only move on the coloured boxes (grey, green, yellow and red).

Did you know?

There are mazes in the real world, too.

- A maize maze is cut from a field of living maize (corn). They are usually grown as a tourist attraction.

- Hampton Court maze is a hedge maze in the grounds of Hampton Court Palace.

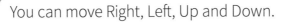

You can move Right, Left, Up and Down.

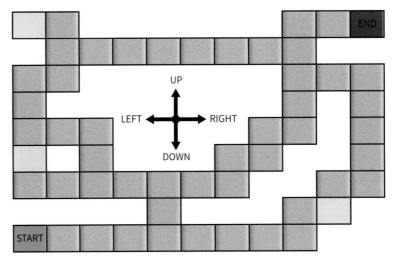

Key word

Sequence: a set of steps or actions that happen in the order they are written.

Activity 2.1

Write a **sequence** to move from 'START' to the red box that says 'END'.

You can only use the commands Right, Left, Up and Down, and the number of the steps to move. For example, Right 4 will move you four spaces to the right.

Activity 2.2

There are three yellow squares on the maze.

Change the sequence so you visit all of the yellow boxes, then go to the 'END' box.

Activity 2.3

Draw your own maze. You can do this on paper or on a computer.

Ask a friend to find their way through your maze. Ask them to write a sequence to get from the start to the end.

Skill 3

Creating a flowchart

Knowing how to create **flowcharts** will help you to show how to order sequences of instructions.

A flowchart is a diagram that shows a sequence of instructions.

It has:

- a Start box, to tell you where you begin
- a Stop box, to tell you where to stop
- **process** boxes, to tell you what to do - these are the instructions
- arrows to tell you which box to look at next.

Each box has a special shape as shown.

The arrows tell you the **order** in which to carry out the instructions.

Key words

Flowchart: a series of boxes, connected with arrows.

Process: an action that performs a task, or changes something.

Order: the way items are arranged.

Activity 3.1

Look at the flowchart.

Follow the instructions.

Begin at the box 'Start'. The arrow tells you to go to the first rectangle. Follow the arrows and do each process.

Did you get it correct?

You should have:

- stood up
- then sat down
- then clapped your hands three times
- then stood up again
- then walked forward two steps.

Activity 3.2

Find the sequence you wrote to get through the maze in **Skill 2**.

Write your sequence as a flowchart.

Swap your flowchart with a friend so they can check that it works.

Working with angles

The amount you can turn is called an angle. These are measured in degrees.

You should already know about full, half and quarter turns.

Turn	Angle
Full turn	360 degrees
Half turn	180 degrees
Quarter turn	90 degrees

Activity 4.1

Look at the maze from **Skill 2** again.

Imagine you are standing in the 'START' square and you are facing towards the grey boxes. You can move forward a number of boxes. You can turn left, or right or at an angle.

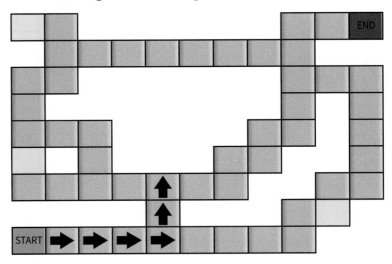

For example:

FORWARD 4
LEFT 90 DEGREES
FORWARD 2

The image shows where you are after this sequence.

Write the rest of the sequence to complete the maze.

Activity 4.2

There are lots of different angles, all the numbers between 0 and 360.

Half of a 90 degree turn is 45 degrees.

Stand up and turn half way to 90 degrees (half of a quarter turn).

45°

Did you know?

Angles are important and you will learn about these in mathematics, too.

Activity 4.3

Look at this new maze.

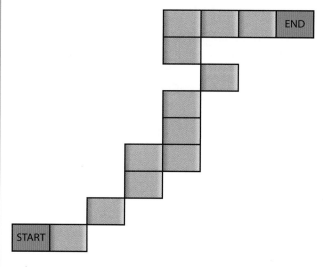

Where two boxes are touching at a corner, you need to turn 45 degrees and then move forward.

Imagine you are standing in the 'START' box facing towards the first grey box. These instructions will get you to the second grey box:

FORWARD 1
LEFT 45 DEGREES
FORWARD 1

Write a sequence to complete the maze.

Key words

Scratch: a piece of software that lets you create programs using blocks to control Sprites.

Sprite: an object or character in Scratch that you can control and add code to. For example:

Tip

Make sure you save your program regularly. Click on **File**, then **Save**. Give your file an appropriate name.

Moving a Sprite forward

You have been writing instructions to move around in a maze. You can now write a computer program to do that using **Scratch**.

Scratch is a program that lets you control objects or characters (**Sprites**).

You can make Sprites move by using program code – these are blocks that you drag into place.

When you open Scratch it should look like this:

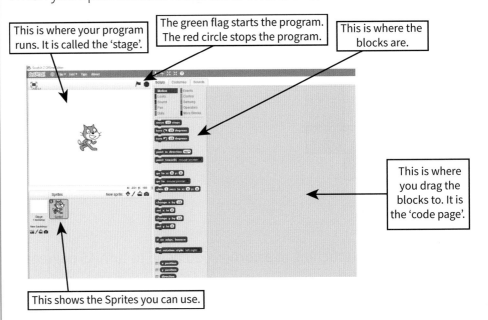

This is where your program runs. It is called the 'stage'.

The green flag starts the program. The red circle stops the program.

This is where the blocks are.

This is where you drag the blocks to. It is the 'code page'.

This shows the Sprites you can use.

Activity 5.1

You are going to make the cat Sprite move forward when the green flag is clicked

1 Click on your cat Sprite.
2 Choose the **Events** menu.
3 Drag the block **when clicked** to the code page.

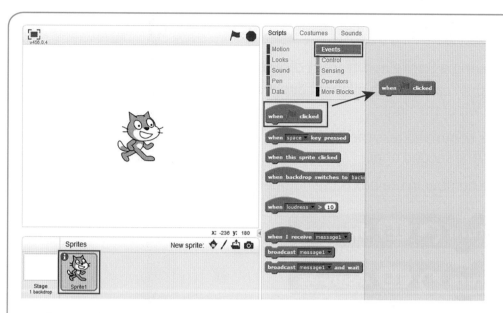

4   Choose the **Motion** menu.

5   Drag 'move 10 steps' to the code page. Put it under the 'green flag'
    block. It will lock into place.

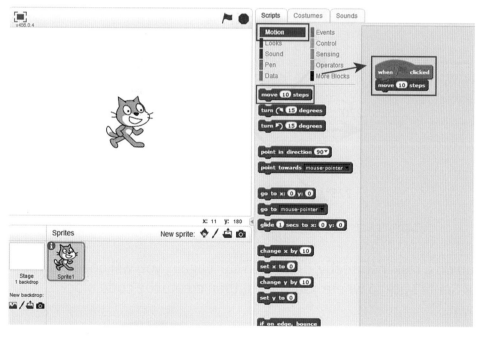

Click the green flag and watch what happens.

Activity 5.2

Change the number of steps.

What happens if you put in 20? Or 50? Or 100?

Tip

If your Sprite
starts to move
off the stage, you
can move it back
by clicking on
it and dragging
it to where you
want it to be.

Tip

You can find the 'turn' blocks in the **Motion** menu. Drag the block to the right hand side, and put it under your other block(s).

Tip

The Sprite will turn in the direction the arrow shows. The larger the number, the larger the turn.

Tip

'Point in direction' lets you tell your Sprite which way to face. It's a different way of making it turn.

The block is in the **Motion** menu, drag it to the right hand side and put it under your other block(s).

Moving a Sprite in different directions

A Sprite can move in different directions by using angles and turning to the left or the right.

This command tells the Sprite to turn to the right (the first one), or the left (the second one).

The number in the box is the number of degrees you want to turn.

If you want your Sprite to turn left 90 degrees, choose the second option and change the number to 90.

This diagram shows the most common angles you will need to use.

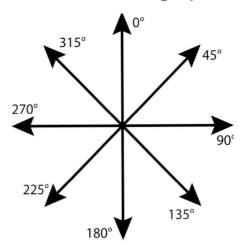

If you do a task incorrectly, or want to start again, you will need to drag your Sprite back to where you want it, then create the code block shown.

The green flag means it will run when you click the green flag. 'Point in direction 90' will make your Sprite turn to face to the right.

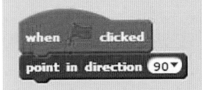

Activity 6.1

Make the Sprite:

- move 100 steps
- turn left 90 degrees
- move another 100 steps.

Your code should look like this:

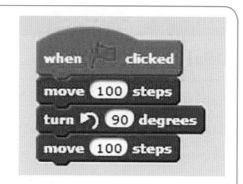

Activity 6.2

Make the Sprite move in a square.

- Move 100 steps.
- Turn left 90 degrees.
- Move 100 steps.
- Turn left 90 degrees.
- Move 100 steps.
- Turn left 90 degrees.
- Move 100 steps.

These instructions might run so fast that you can't see the Sprite move. You can put 'Wait' commands between each instruction. This will slow it down.

'Wait' is found in the **Control** menu of commands.

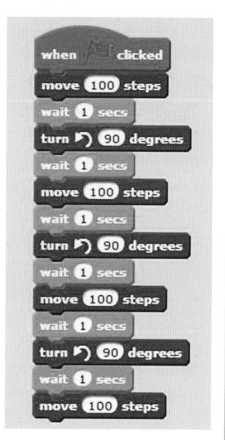

Activity 6.3

Make the Sprite move in a square, turning to the right instead of the left.

Activity 6.4

Make the Sprite move at different angles.

Type in different numbers and see what the Sprite does.

Did it do what you thought it would?

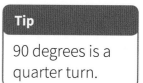

Tip

90 degrees is a quarter turn.

Key word

Debug: finding an error in a program so you can fix it.

Tip

Click the green flag and watch what happens. Where did he move to? Which command was wrong? Can you fix it?

Tip

Select the 'turn' block with the arrow pointing left, then type 90 in the box.

Did you know?

One of the first ever computers stopped working because the programmer found a fly in it! The fly had to be removed because the computer didn't work so had to be 'debugged'.

Debugging

Programs almost never work first time. That's ok, it does not mean you have failed.

It means you need to work out what went wrong, then fix it.

Finding out what went wrong is called **debugging**.

Activity 7.1

Open the Scratch file 'debugging.sb2' that your teacher will give you.

Dino the dinosaur wants to:

- move to the right 100 steps
- turn left 90 degrees
- move forward 50 steps.

The program doesn't work. Can you work out why?

Click on the Restart button to make Dino move back to the start.

Activity 7.2

Open the Scratch file 'debugging2.sb2' that your teacher will give you. Kim the dragon wants to:

- move to the right 100 steps
- turn so they are facing down (you need to work out the angle)
- move forward 100 steps.

The program doesn't work. Can you work out why?

Click on the Restart button to make Kim move back to the start.

Activity 7.3

Open the Scratch file 'debugging3.sb2' that your teacher will give you.

Imani the reindeer wants to move to touch the Earth. The program doesn't work. Can you work out why?

Click on the Restart button to make Imani move back to the start.

Scenario

Escape from the castle

You have a mission! Your friends, Alexis and Amirah are trapped in a castle and you need to help them to escape. What will you need to think about to get them to the exit?

Alexis and Amirah enter the room at the 'START'. They need to get to the key, and then the 'EXIT'.

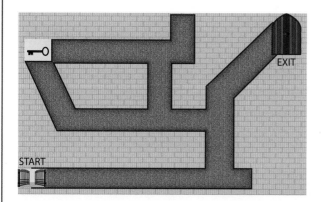

Activity 1

Draw a flowchart to get Alexis and Amirah to the key, then to 'EXIT'.

You can **predict** how many steps you think they will need to move. You can change this later in your program.

Activity 2

Swap your flowchart with a friend.

Follow your friend's flowchart. Will it get Alexis and Amirah out of the room?

Activity 3

Open the Scratch file 'castle1.sb2' that your teacher will give you.

Use your flowchart to move Alexis and Amirah to the key, then the exit.

Click on the apple to restart the program. This moves Alexis and Amirah back to the start.

You can ignore the code that is already in the program, this resets it for you.

Key word

Prediction: working out what might happen, before actually doing it.

Tip

Remember to think about which way you want the Sprite to turn, left or right. Pretend you are the Sprite; which way would you want to turn?

Activity 4

Alexis and Amirah escaped the first room but are now trapped again!

Open the Scratch file 'castle2.sb2' that your teacher will give you. Do not run the program.

What do you think will happen? Read the commands. Predict what will happen.

Will Alexis and Amirah get to the exit?

Activity 5

Run the program 'castle2.sb2' that your teacher will give you. Alexis and Amirah did not get to the exit.

Debug the program. Why didn't Alexis and Amirah escape?

Change the code to help Alexis and Amirah escape.

Tip

The red apple will reset the program and move the characters back to the start.

Challenge

Activity 1

You can make your Sprite 'speak'. Speech commands are in the section **Looks**.

Add the block 'say'.

Type your message in the first box.

Type how many seconds you want the message to appear on screen.

At the start of the program make your Sprite say "I'm ready, let's go".

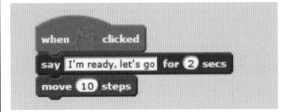

Add messages in one of your programs.

Activity 2

There is a 'think' option.

Put a think command into a program.

What is the difference between think and say?

Final project – Clip Clop the horse

Open the file 'Zoo.sb2' that your teacher will give you.

Clip Clop the Horse is visiting a zoo and wants to see all the animals there.

He starts in the white box.

He can only see the animals when he is touching the red circles.

Clip Clop wants to see the tigers first.

Activity 1

Draw a flowchart to move Clip Clop to the red dot next to the tigers.

Activity 2

Swap your flowchart with a friend.

Use your friend's flowchart to work out whether Clip Clop will get to see the tigers.

Activity 3

Use your flowchart to create a program to move Clip Clop to the tigers.

The Restart button will take Clip Clop back to the start.

Activity 4

Change your program.

After seeing the tigers, Clip Clop wants to visit:

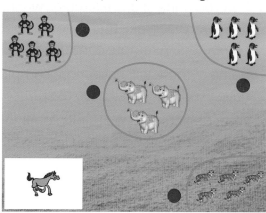

- the penguins
- then the monkeys
- and finally, the elephants.

If your program does not work the first time, don't worry! Debug it and solve the problem.

> **Tip**
>
> If you click on Restart, you will need to click on Clip Clop again to see his code.

Reflection

Think about the following:

1 What sequences of instructions are you given to follow? These might not be written as a flowchart, but even your teacher will give you sequences such as:

Get out your pens.

Open your book.

Start by writing a title for your work today, etc.

Think of a sequence you have been given and write it below. Compare your sequence to another person's.

_____

_____

_____

_____

_____

_____

_____

_____

_____

_____

2 Can you think of any examples where objects are given instructions to follow that make them move? Robots that build objects like cars, or computers? A remote controlled car?

Some of these will have more complicated instructions than those you have used, but we all have to start somewhere!

What objects can you think of that follow instructions? Write them below and share them with your class.

_____

_____

_____

_____

_____

_____

_____

_____

_____

3 How many things in your house work by following instructions? Write them below and share them with your class.

_____

_____

_____

_____

_____

_____

	In this module, you will learn how to:	Pass/Merit	Done?
1	Use buttons, menus and indexes to navigate and find information	P	
2	Use keywords to search for information	P	
3	Show evidence of your research	P	
4	Choose suitable keywords	M	
5	Choose suitable results.	M	

In this module you are going to develop searching skills to help you work towards your final project. In this project you will be creating information sheets about two species of endangered animals: polar bears and one other species. The choice is yours! You will need to search for information about both animals in order to make your information sheet interesting and fun.

You will also learn:

- what web browsers and search engines are and the difference between them
- how to use questions and keywords to look for information
- how to keep yourself safe when using a search engine
- how to show evidence of the research you have done.

Before you start

You should:

- know what a search engine is
- have used a search engine before.

Introduction

How well can you use a search engine?

It can be fun to search for **information** on the **World Wide Web** and learn about new and interesting topics.

You can also quickly and easily search for information that you need to complete tasks.

To search for information on the World Wide Web, you need two pieces of software: a **web browser** and a **search engine**.

It is important to be able to use a search engine effectively and to be able to select the best **search results** for the information you need.

Key words

Information: facts that you can learn about something or someone.

World Wide Web (WWW): the collection of webpages that are accessed by using the internet.

Web browser: a piece of software that retrieves (fetches), translates and displays webpages.

Search engine: a program that is used to search large databases that contain websites from the World Wide Web.

Search results: the list of links to webpages that are given by a search engine.

Key word

E-safety:
staying safe while using the internet.

Stay safe!

The world wide web can be fun and is full of lots of interesting and entertaining webpages. However, you may also come across some dangers. You need to make sure that you can recognise these dangers and keep yourself safe when using the internet. This is called **e-safety**.

When using search engines to find information, you may also find information that is offensive or illegal (against the law). You should not look at this information. To make sure that you do not look at any harmful information, you can follow these guidelines:

- Make sure that you choose your search words carefully. Any misspellings or general search words that don't provide enough information, may give you results that are not useful or possibly harmful.
- Look out for any warnings given when opening a webpage that it may contain harmful information.
- Remember that not all search results will be reliable. Only click on the links for well-known and reliable websites.
- Remember that the first results may not always be the best ones. Some companies pay to have their results at the top. You can see which ones these are as they may have 'Ad' or 'Sponsored' next to them.

Your safety when using the internet is very important. You should make sure that you are careful each time you follow a link from a search result. Choose wisely!

If you do find a webpage that has harmful information, tell your teacher straight away. You will not be in trouble.

Skill 1

Web browsers

A web browser is a piece of software that shows you webpages from the World Wide Web, so that you can read them.

Webpages are sent across the internet in a computer language such as Hypertext Mark-up Language (HTML). The web browser translates this into a language that you can read.

Popular examples of web browsers include:

- Google Chrome
- Safari
- Microsoft Edge
- Firefox.

Each web browser has four main parts that you may need to use.

The four main parts are:

- the Address bar
- the **Forward** button
- the **Back** button
- the **Refresh** button.

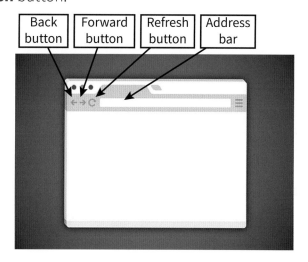

Did you know?

A web address is sometimes called a URL (Universal Resource Locator).

Tip

You can find a link on a page by moving the mouse around the screen until the ▶ changes to a 🖑.

The **Back** button allows you to navigate back to any webpages that you want to return to.

If you have used the **Back** button to go back to a webpage, you can use the **Forward** button to go forward to a webpage you have just visited.

The **Refresh** button allows you to **reload** a webpage. This can be useful if a webpage hasn't **loaded** properly. It is also useful if a website has information on it that will change and be updated. When you use the **Refresh** button, it will reload the web page you are on and show any updates that have been made.

The Address bar is where you type the website address of a webpage you want to visit. Each webpage has its own, unique address. The web address for NASA is www.nasa.gov. It can be shortened (making it easier to type) by missing off the 'www'.

Activity 1.1
Open your web browser.

Type the website address www.nasa.gov/kidsclub into the address bar.

Press Enter.

Activity 1.2
Click on a **link** to another page from the home page.

Activity 1.3
Click the **Back** button to go back to the home page.

Activity 1.4
Click the **Forward** button to return to the other page.

Activity 1.5
Click the **Refresh** button to reload the page.

Well done! You have now used the main features of a web browser.

Skill 2

Search engines

A search engine allows you to search the World Wide Web for information.

There are many search engines: Google, Bing, DuckDuckGo, Yahoo and Kiddle are some you might use.

A search engine works like a textbook, just on a much larger scale.

If you open a textbook at the back, you will normally find an **index**.

If you want to find certain information in the book, you can use the index to find the page number for the information. You can then go to the correct page in the book.

Most search engines will have a search bar that you can type text into to create a search.

All the websites that are available on the World Wide Web are stored in a **database.** A search engine can be used to search through the database to find the information that is needed.

Activity 2.1

Open your chosen search engine.

Type the name of your country into the search bar. Press Enter, or there may be a search icon such as Q that you can click.

Look at the search results that appear on the search results page.

Identify and click on a link that will take you to information about the capital city of your country.

Key words

Index: a list of key words or topics that is normally in alphabetical order.

Database: a collection of information that is organised so that it can be easily searched and accessed.

WATCH OUT!

You should only click on links that look trustworthy and age appropriate.

Keyword: an important word (or words) which summarise the information you want to find.

Keyword-based search

One way to search the World Wide Web is a **keyword** search.

When you want to find out information about a topic you can think about the keywords that may be useful in your search.

Activity 3.1

You are going to find out about a planet called Pluto.

Open your search engine.

Type in 'Pluto'.

Look at the search results that appear on the search results page.

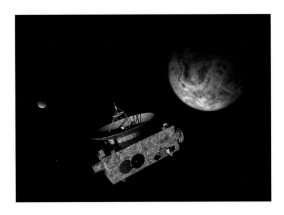

Now type 'Pluto + solar system' into the search bar.

Look at the search results that appear on the search results page.

Now type in 'Pluto + solar system + planet'.

Look at the search results that appear on the search results page.

Were the results always the same? Did adding more keywords give you more information?

_____

Activity 3.2

What other keywords might help you with this search?

_____

Tip

The '+' sign tells the search engine that you only want to see search results that have all the keywords in them.

Activity 3.3

You might want to look up information, but want the search engine <u>not</u> to show you certain search results as they will not be useful.

You may want to find out about the cartoon character Pluto and not the planet. You can use a keyword search to do this.

Open your search engine.

Type 'Pluto' into the search engine.

Look at search results that appear on the search results page.

Type 'Pluto + cartoon character–planet' into the search engine.

Look at search results that appear on the search results page.

Did you see a difference?

The search results should show more results about the cartoon character Pluto now.

Activity 3.4

What other keywords could you include that the search engine should <u>not</u> show searches for?

Tip

The '–' should tell the search engine not to show any searches that contain the word 'planet'.

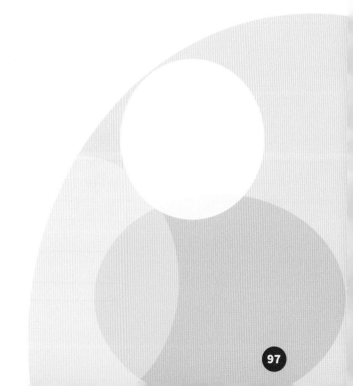

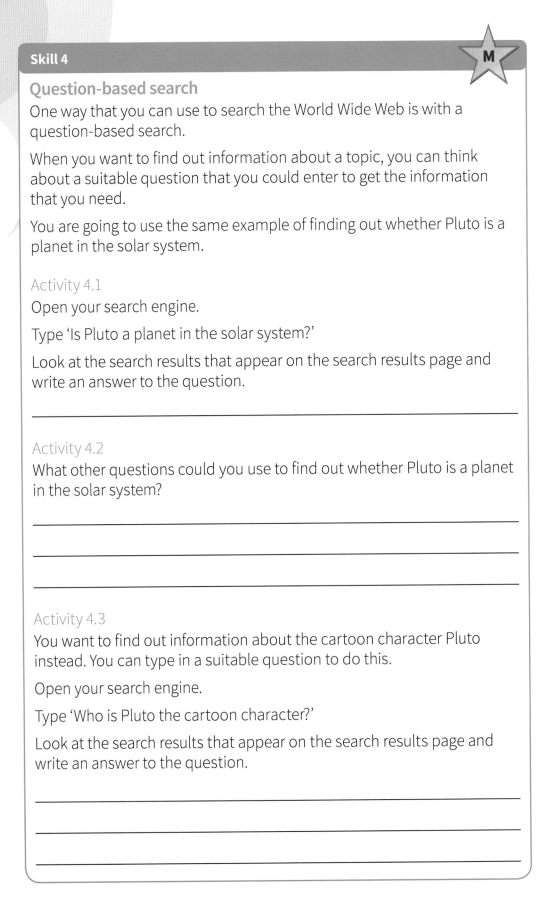

Skill 4

Question-based search

One way that you can use to search the World Wide Web is with a question-based search.

When you want to find out information about a topic, you can think about a suitable question that you could enter to get the information that you need.

You are going to use the same example of finding out whether Pluto is a planet in the solar system.

Activity 4.1

Open your search engine.

Type 'Is Pluto a planet in the solar system?'

Look at the search results that appear on the search results page and write an answer to the question.

_____

Activity 4.2

What other questions could you use to find out whether Pluto is a planet in the solar system?

_____

_____

_____

Activity 4.3

You want to find out information about the cartoon character Pluto instead. You can type in a suitable question to do this.

Open your search engine.

Type 'Who is Pluto the cartoon character?'

Look at the search results that appear on the search results page and write an answer to the question.

_____

_____

_____

Skill 5

Is a source trustworthy?

There is a lot of information available on the World Wide Web, but is it all useful? Is all the information correct?

Information is more likely to be correct if you get it from a **reputable** source. (Sources may contain resources such as different types of files or other links. A resource is only as good as the source it comes from, however!)

There are a few pieces of information that will help you work out whether a source is trustworthy or not.

The author

If you know that a source comes from an author who has given lots of correct information in the past, then you can be more certain that the information will be correct this time.

Who can edit the source?

If a source can be **edited** by a lot of people, this can help give more information about the topic.

However, it can also mean that it might contain errors as the information may not have been properly checked.

Activity 5.1

List all the adults who tell you information.

_____

_____

_____

Is the information they tell you correct?

Who are the most trustworthy out of the adults you listed?

_____

_____

_____

Activity 5.2

Open your web browser.

Type www.nasa.gov/kidsclub into the address bar.

Click on 'Find out who is on the Space Station'.

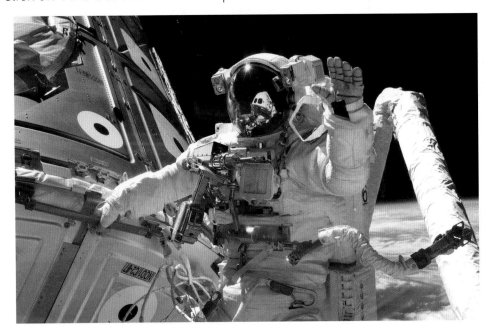

Activity 5.3

On a piece of paper, write down one piece of information you found about one of the astronauts.

Pass this onto someone else. You should get one from one of your classmates.

Now write down another piece of information you found out.

Do this three more times but on one occasion, write down a false piece of information.

Find your original piece of paper.

Can you work out which piece of information is incorrect?

Tip

There might be more than one!

Scenario

My country

You have been given a research project to complete. You need to prepare a report about your country that must include the following:

- where it is on the earth
- the climate
- the size and shape
- the population
- five other facts.

You will need to search for the information on the World Wide Web to write your research report.

Activity 1

Use a book and look in the index to find out about your country.

Activity 2

Type the name of your country into a search engine and see what search results appear.

What were the top three search results?

Did any of them give you the information you needed?

Activity 3

Type the name of the continent your country is in into a search engine and see what search results appear.

Are the search results different this time?

Is it easy to see a source that would provide the answer?

Has this produced a better list of search results?

Activity 4

Type 'Where is [and then insert the name of your country]' into a search engine and see what search results appear.

Are the search results different this time?

Is it easy to see a source that would provide an answer?

Can you think of another question you could use?

Do you think it was easier to search with the keywords or the question?

Activity 5

Think of some keywords to find out about the climate in your country.

Type your keywords into a search engine and see what search results appear.

What were the top three search results?

Did it look like any of them would tell you information about climate?

Activity 6

Think of a question to help you find out about the climate in your country.

Type your question into a search engine and see what search results appear.

Are the search results different this time?

Is it easy to see a webpage that would provide information about the climate?

Do you think it was easier to search with the keywords or the question?

Activity 7

Use the skills you have mastered to find out about the size and shape of your country and its population. Then think of five facts of your own to investigate.

Can you identify a search result that would be a trustworthy source?

Can you think of anything else that would help identify whether a source is trustworthy?

Activity 8

Did you find it easier to search for information on your chosen country in a book or using a search engine? Why is that?

Challenge

Referencing a source

When you use information that you have found on the World Wide Web in your own work, it is very important that you include where the information came from. This is called **referencing**. If you don't do this, you could be accused of **plagiarism**.

The best way to do this is to add a **bibliography** to your work. Each source in the bibliography should include:

- the website's address
- the author of the website (if this information is available)
- the date and time you accessed the website for the information.

For example, a website that you may have used when finding out whether Pluto is a planet is the NASA website. A reference for this would be:

Website address: https://solarsystem.nasa.gov/planets/pluto, author Bill Dunford, accessed on 10/05/2018 at 10:00am.

Activity 1

Create a bibliography of the sources that you used to find the information for the report about your country.

Key words

Reference: identifying and listing a source that has been used in a piece of work.

Plagiarism: copying someone else's work without referencing it.

Bibliography: a list of sources that you have used in your work.

Final project – Researching endangered species

You and a partner are going to complete an exciting project of your own using your new searching skills.

You are going to prepare an information sheet for your class about two endangered species:

- polar bears
- one other animal of your own choice.

You need to find out:

- what their scientific name is
- where they live
- what they eat
- how long they live for

- what the difference in weight is between the average male and the average female
- what sense they use to detect their prey
- at what time of the year their babies are born
- what is affecting their survival.

Activity 1
Research a list of endangered animals and choose the second animal for your information sheet.

Activity 2
Research the information that you need to find out for the polar bear. You could try using both keyword and question-based searches.

Activity 3
Open a new document and type the information you have researched about polar bears. You might want to make some notes of the information as you do your research.

Activity 4
Save your document with a suitable filename.

Activity 5
Research the information that you need to find out for your second chosen animal.

Activity 6
Type the information about your chosen animal into your document. Save the document again.

Activity 7
Search for suitable images of a polar bear and your chosen animal. Save each image.

Activity 8
Insert the images of the polar bear and your chosen animal into your information sheet, in a suitable place.

Tip

It might be useful for you to keep a list of the websites you visit during your research.

Reflection

Think about the following:

1 When you created your presentation on endangered species, did you use keyword-based searches or question-based searches? Why did you choose this method?

_____

_____

_____

_____

2 Do you think this method gave you the best results?

_____

_____

_____

_____

3 How did you keep yourself safe when using the search engine and selecting your sources?

_____

_____

_____

_____

Starting email 6

	In this module, you will learn how to:	Pass/Merit	Done?
1	Create and send email messages	P	
2	Reply to email messages	P	
3	Collect and read email messages	P	
4	Use email folders	M	
5	Forward email messages and copy to another recipient.	M	

Did you know?

The 'e' in email stands for 'electronic'.

In this module you are going to develop email skills to help you work towards your final project. This project will be working with friends to write a story that will be written and sent using email.

Did you know?

Email was first used in the 1960s in a university in the USA.

You will also learn:

- how to send the same email to different people
- how to reply to your emails
- how to format your emails (for example, change the font type, size and colour)
- how to put your emails into folders
- how to stay safe when using emails.

Before you start

You should:

- know what email is, and what it does. You might not have used it yet.
- have an email account
- know how to log into your email account
- be able to control a pointer on a computer and click on buttons.

Introduction

Email is electronic mail.

To send and receive emails you need an email account.

You can get an email address from a variety of **email providers**. You could use Gmail or Microsoft Outlook for example.

In this module you will use Gmail. All the providers have similar tools, but the buttons might be in different places.

When you get an email account, you get an **email address**. No-one else in the world will have the same email address, it is **unique**. If they had the same email address they would receive your emails, and you would receive their emails.

Look at this example email address:

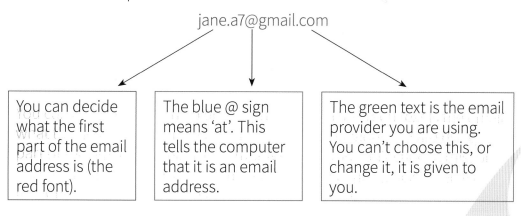

jane.a7@gmail.com

| You can decide what the first part of the email address is (the red font). | The blue @ sign means 'at'. This tells the computer that it is an email address. | The green text is the email provider you are using. You can't choose this, or change it, it is given to you. |

Someone else might already have the email address that you choose. You will need to change the first part (the red). For example, you could put meaningful numbers at the end, such as your favourite number.

Stay safe!

When using the internet it is important that you stay safe. This includes using email. This is called **e-safety**.

There are rules you must follow to stay safe when using email:

1 If you receive an email from someone you don't know, tell an appropriate adult (your teacher or parent/carer) and delete the email. Do <u>not</u> open the email.

2 Carefully check who you receive emails from. If the address is not exactly the same as the one you are expecting, do <u>not</u> open the email.

3 <u>Never</u> send emails to people you do not know without first checking with an appropriate adult.

4 <u>Never</u> enter your email address on any websites without first checking with an appropriate adult.

5 <u>Never</u> tell anyone the password you use to **connect** to your email.

6 <u>Never</u> open **attachments** from people you don't know. An attachment is a file that comes with the email. You will know if there is an attachment because the email will have a paper clip icon next to it.

7 Send a **carbon copy (cc)** of emails you send to an appropriate adult.

Your teacher will tell you who to expect emails from. This could be people in your school, or people in other schools.

Skill 1

Writing a new email

You are going to send an email to your teacher. The email will be about your friends and family.

This is what an email account looks like.

> **Compose** lets you write a new email. Some providers might say **New** instead of **Compose**.

> This is where emails will appear. You can see that there are no emails here yet.

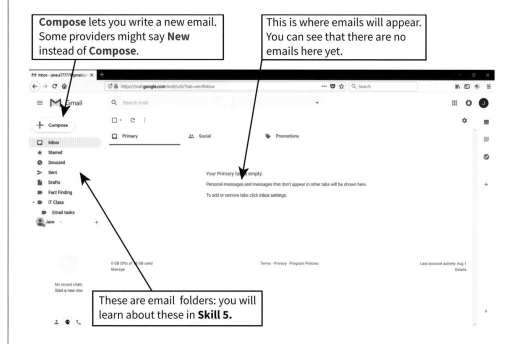

> These are email folders: you will learn about these in **Skill 5.**

Activity 1.1

First, log into your email account.

To **compose** a new email, click on the **Compose** button.

In Gmail, a new window appears with the title New Message.

Key word

Compose: to create something new. For example, composing an email means writing a new email.

Subject line: the place where you can write the introduction, or title to the email. It is what people view in their inbox so they know what your email is about.

Recipient: the person who receives the email.

Activity 1.2

The **subject line** is where you write the title of your email. This is a short sentence so the **recipient** will know what the email is about.

Click in the box with the word 'Subject' in.

Type: 'My family and friends'.

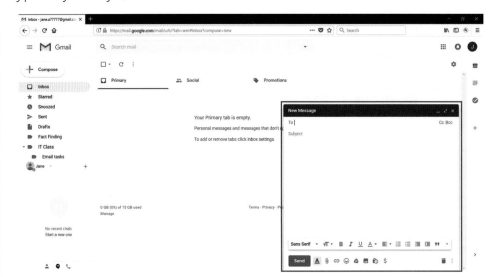

Activity 1.3

The box below 'Subject' is where you type your message.

Write a message to your teacher in the email you composed for **Activity 1.1**.

Tell your teacher some interesting facts about your family and your friends.

Start and finish it with an appropriate greeting.

Here is an example email:

Dear Mr Shakespeare,

I would like to tell you about my family and friends. I live at home with my mum and dad. I have one older sister called Rebecca.

My best friend at school is called Sarah and she is in the same class as me. I have lots of other friends, like Alex and Kamran and Jay.

Best wishes,

Jane

The image shows the text in the new message.

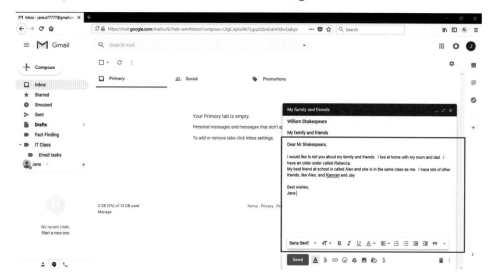

You need to make sure your message is appropriate for the recipient. Emails need to start and finish appropriately. This is called email **etiquette**. Some example rules are shown below.

- Your email should start with a greeting (for example, Dear / Hello) and finish with a greeting (for example, Thank you / Best wishes) – exactly like you would when writing a letter.
- Check your spelling and grammar before sending your email.
- Make sure you have included a subject and it matches your message.
- Use a simple, readable font (do not use lots of different colours, a fancy font, or put whole words in capitals – this is shouting).

Skill 2

Entering the recipient's address and sending the email

When you have written your email, you will need to add the recipient's email address.

Activity 2.1

You need to know your teacher's email address. They will either tell you this or write it on a board so you can see it.

Click in the box next to To.

Type your teacher's email address in the space.

Copy it carefully and make sure:

- you use the right symbols, for example full stops (.) and dashes (-)
- your spellings are correct
- you have included the @ sign.

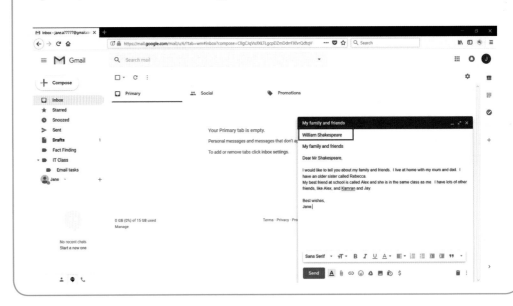

Activity 2.2

Now your email is finished, you can send it.

Click on 'Send'.

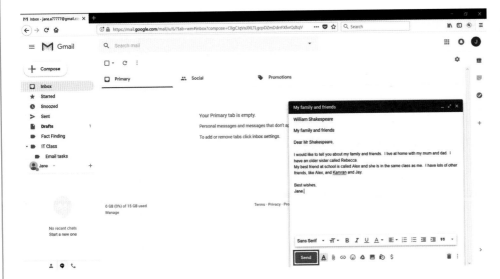

When you are connected to your email account, the email will be sent straight away. This is an **online send**.

Sometimes you can write emails without connecting. When this happens your email will be saved in the drafts folder, or **outbox**. It sends when you next connect. This is an **offline send**.

Key words

Online send: when you are connected to your email account and an email is sent straight away.

Outbox: an email folder that stores an email after you click on 'Send', until the email provider sends it.

Offline send: when you write and send an email, but are not connected to your email account.

Key word

Address book: a place in your email account where you can store the email addresses of people you know.

Skill 3

Accessing the address book

Email accounts have **address books** that store people's names and email addresses. This means you don't need to remember every email address.

Your teacher will have added email addresses to your address book already.

Activity 3.1

Compose a new email.

Click on the word 'To'. This will open your address book.

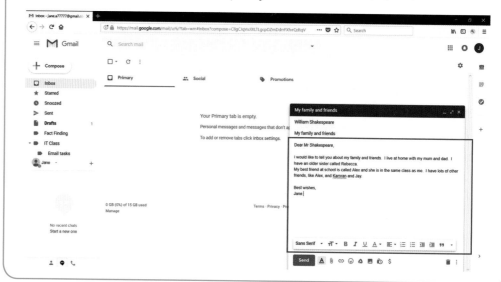

Activity 3.2

The new window will show you all the people your teacher has added to your address book.

Click on the box next to the person you want to send an email to.

Click on 'Select'.

Tip

Follow the instructions for **Skill 2, Activity 2.2**.

Activity 3.3

Send your email.

Skill 4

Reading and replying to an email

When you connect to your email account, new email messages will show in your **inbox**.

Next to Inbox it will show the number of new messages you have. The new emails are in bold.

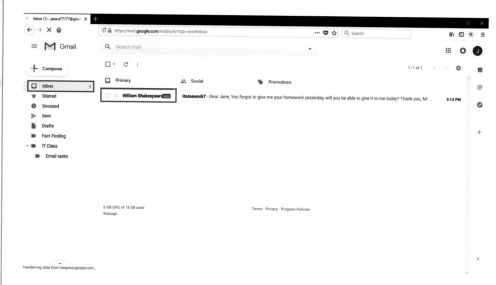

Activity 4.1

The inbox tells you a lot about the emails you have **received**.

| The person who sent you the email. | The subject. | The first part of the email. |

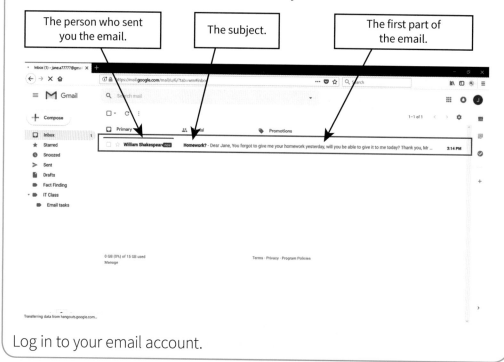

Log in to your email account.

Have you received any messages?

If you have, how do you know:

- whether these are new emails?

  _____

- who are they from?

  _____

- what are they about?

  _____

Activity 4.2

Click on one of your new emails.

You can now read the whole message and reply to it.

Click on **Reply** in the box below the message. Or click on the arrow.

This will prepare a reply to the person who sent you the email.

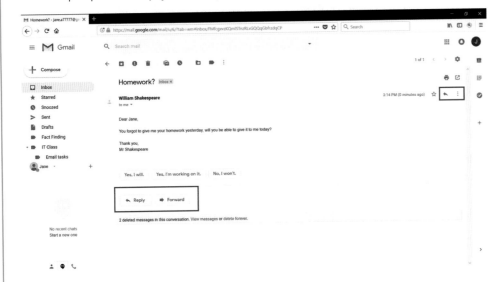

Write your message in the box.

Then, when you have checked it, click on 'Send'.

You do not need to write the recipient's email address. Reply does this for you.

Key word

Reply: this is when you receive an email and then send one back to the person who wrote it. The email they sent is usually included in the reply.

The 'Re' which is added to the subject line when you reply to emails comes from Latin.

It means "in the matter of".

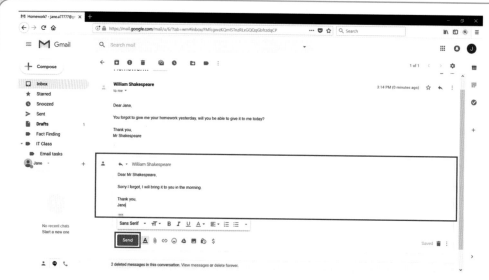

The subject will not change, but it will now start with Re:

Skill 5

Using email folders

A **folder** is a place where you can store specific messages.

You can have lots of different folders. Each folder has its own unique name.

Your email account will come with some folders already set up. Some email providers might use different names, and some might not have all these folders.

Folder	Description
Inbox	This is where new emails arrive. It also stores the emails you have read and not moved to a different folder.
Outbox	When you click on send, the email goes to the outbox. Once the email has been sent by your provider, it disappears from the outbox.

Folder	Description
Sent Mail	The emails you have sent are stored in this folder.
Drafts	When you start writing an email, it is saved to drafts.
	This is a backup, in case you accidentally delete the email you are writing.
	You can save an email as a draft, for example, when you have started to write it, but want to finish later.
Deleted items (Bin/ Trash)	You can delete emails you don't want or need.
	These are moved to the Trash folder.
	They stay there until you delete them from the folder.
	When they are deleted from here you cannot get them back.

The folders are on the left-hand side.

Key words

Sent mail: this is a folder in your email account where all the messages you have sent to other people are stored.

Draft: an email that is saved before it is sent, so you can change it in the future.

Activity 5.1
Click on each of the folders in your email account. Are there any emails in them?

Activity 5.2
Start writing a new email. Look at the Drafts folder – does this change? Is your email saved as a draft?

Activity 5.3

Look in your Sent folder. How many emails have you sent to people?

Activity 5.4

Look in your Deleted items folder. Are there any emails in the folder? Do you need to permanently delete any of these emails?

If so, delete them. If you do not have any yet, then you can do this at a later time.

Key word

Forward: this is when you receive an email, and then send the same email to one or more people.

Skill 6

Forward email messages

You might receive an email that you want to send on to someone else. This is called **forwarding**.

Activity 6.1

Open the email you want to forward.

Click on 'Forward'.

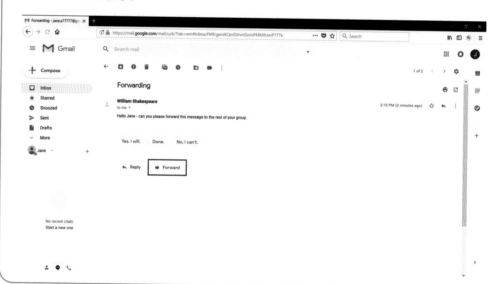

The text you were sent is also in the new email.

Enter the recipient's email address here.

Enter your text to add to the email here above the Forwarded message.

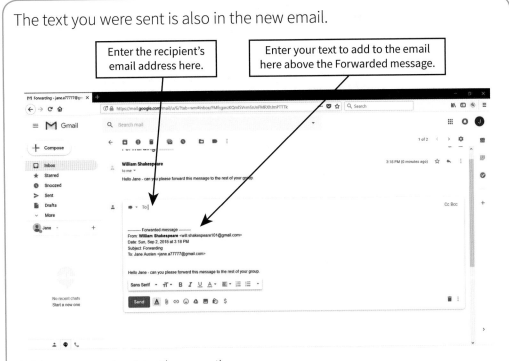

Add your own text to the email.

Enter the email address (or use your address book) of the person you want to forward the email to.

Click on 'Send' when you're ready.

Activity 6.2

You can send a carbon copy (cc) of an email to a second person.

The To recipient gets the email and the cc recipient also gets it.

You can use cc when the cc person needs to know you have sent the email, or if it has information in it that they need to know.

Click in the To box.

Click on the **cc** button on the right hand side.

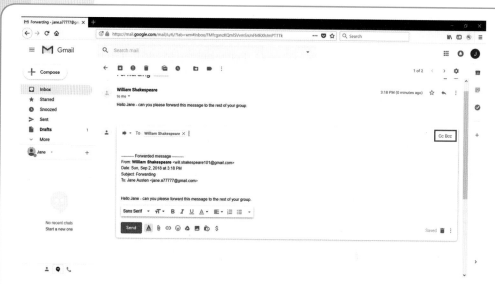

Add your text to the email.

Click in the new cc space.

Enter the email address of the cc recipient (or use your address book).

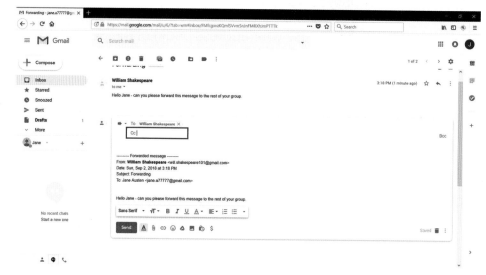

If you are forwarding an email to a new person, it is polite to cc in the original person who sent you the email. Then that person knows other people have also seen it.

Scenario

Emailing your hobbies

Your teacher would like to know what your favourite hobbies are, and what you like to do when you are not at school.

Activity 1

Send a new email to your teacher.

Write a message telling them about your favourite hobby (for example, reading or playing sport).

Ask your teacher an appropriate question, for example, "What topic do you like teaching the most?"

Make sure you:

1 include a suitable subject
2 start and end your email with an appropriate greeting and ending
3 check your spelling and grammar
4 enter your teacher's correct email address (or use your address book).

Activity 2

Your teacher will reply to your email.

1 Check your email.
2 When you receive the reply, open and read the message.
3 Your teacher should have asked you a question. Reply to their email, answering their question.

Activity 3

1 Write a list of the folders in your email account in a word-processing document.

2 Describe the purpose of each folder.

Activity 4

Your friend would like to read the email your teacher sent to you.

Forward this email to one of your friends.

Cc your teacher into your email so they know who you have sent it to.

Challenge

Adding multiple recipients

Activity 1

It is possible to send one email to lots of different recipients.

Compose a new email.

In the To box enter more than one email address (or select them from your address book).

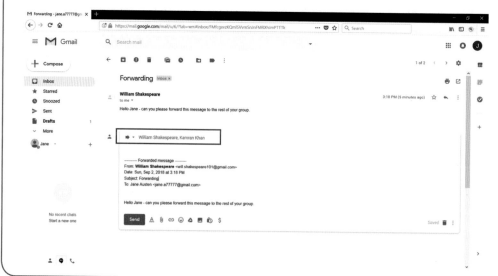

Formatting an email

Activity 2

You can change the **format** of the text you put into an email. You can change lots of things, for example, the **font** style, size and colour.

Highlight the text you want to change by dragging your cursor across the words you want to change.

Click on the **A** button.

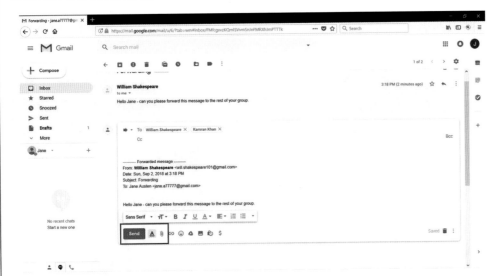

The new toolbar lets you change the font style, size and colour. You can also add bullet points

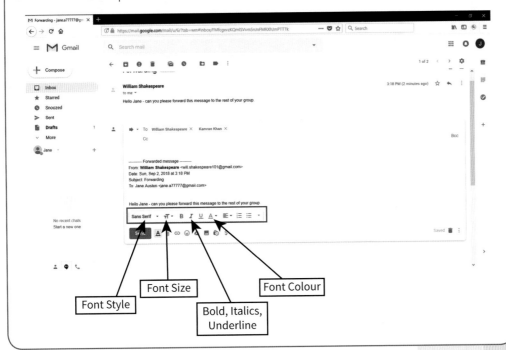

Font Style

Font Size

Font Colour

Bold, Italics, Underline

Key words

Format: change the appearance of the text. For example, formatting the font might mean changing the colour and size.

Font: the design of the text used on a computer, for example, Arial, Times New Roman, Calibri.

Remember: all changes should be appropriate.

If you are writing a formal email, use a sensible font that is not too large, small or decorative, and is black in colour.

Bold, underline and italics are be used to show points that are more important.

Final project – Writing a story in a group

You are going to work together with two friends to write several stories using email.

Make sure the email addresses for your friends are already in your address book.

Your teacher will help you with this.

Activity 1

1 Compose a new email.
2 Write the first couple of sentences of a story.
3 Give your story a title and write it in the subject.
4 Add the address of one friend.
5 Add your teacher as a cc.
6 Send the email.

Activity 2

1 Check your email for new mail.

2 When you receive the start of the story from a friend, open it and read it.

3 Reply to the email.

4 Write new sentence(s) for the next part of the story.

5 Add your teacher as a cc.

6 Send the email.

Activity 3

1 Check your email for new mail.

2 When you receive a reply from your friend, open it and read it.

3 This time, choose 'Forward'.

4 Write new sentence(s) for the next part of the story.

5 Add your second friend's email address.

6 Add your teacher as a cc.

7 Send the email.

Activity 4

Keep on repeating **Activity 3**.

Read each story, then either reply to the email, or forward it to another friend.

Add your own part to the story each time.

Remember to send a carbon copy to your teacher each time.

You should now have several different stories that you have written together as a group.

Reflection

Think about the following:

1 Give three reasons why it is important to stay safe when using email?

_____

_____

_____

_____

2 Give three rules you need to follow to stay safe when using email?

_____

_____

_____

_____

3 How has email changed how people get in touch with each other?

_____

_____

_____

_____